A
REMARKABLE
JOURNEY

The Pillars of St. Mary's. These women, through their vision, wisdom, and courage, represent the spirit and strength of St. Mary's Episcopal School. M. Kirby-Smith '67, Artist. Photo by David Nester.

A Remarkable Journey

by Mary M. Davis

AUGUST HOUSE, INC. PUBLISHERS LITTLE ROCK

Published 1998 by August House, Inc.
P.O. Box 3223, Little Rock, Arkansas 72203,
501-372-5450

Printed in the United States of America

10 9 8 7 6 5 4 3 2 1

Library of Congress Cataloging-in-Publication Data
Davis, Mary M. (Mary McClintock), 1911-
A Remarkable Journey / Mary M. Davis.
        p.   cm.
Includes bibliographical references and index.
ISBN 0-87483-547-X (alk. paper)
1. St. Mary's Episcopal School (Memphis, Tenn.)--History.
I. Title.
LD7501.M437455D38   1998
371.071 '3' 076819--dc21   98-40370
                                                          CIP

Project executive: Ted Parkhurst
Editor: Sarah Scott
Designer: Frances J. Hagen

The paper used in this publication meets the minimum requirements of the
American National Standard for Information Sciences—Permanence of Paper for
Printed Library Materials, ANSI Z39.48-1984

AUGUST HOUSE, INC.   PUBLISHERS   LITTLE ROCK

This book is lovingly dedicated to the community of St. Mary's,
past and present, who have created and sustained
this very special place.

Table of Contents

PREFACE

Everyone has a story to tell. To share our experiences and feelings with others gives us joy. We delight in talking about our past—our dreams, our successes, our disappointments—for stories about the past reveal pictures of ourselves; stories let others have a glimpse of who we really are. Similarly, St. Mary's Episcopal School has a story to tell—a rich, poignant, and sometimes dramatic one that spans 150 years. Because of my long association with and devotion to St. Mary's, I was asked to be the storyteller.

A Remarkable Journey is a story of the first 150 years of St. Mary's existence, revealing the school's dedication to the academic and spiritual education of girls. As I began my research and talked with individuals connected with the past and present of the school, I became increasingly interested in its leaders, the headmasters and principals. A persistent longing urged me to become as closely acquainted as possible with these individuals. It has been a fascinating experience to uncover their strengths, their struggles, their disappointments, and their dreams. Each era has revealed strong leadership, the pursuit of excellence, and a concern and love for the students—all of which are underscored by a deep faith in God. For these reasons, I chose to write this particular history of St. Mary's as a collection of individual portraits, roughly arranged in chronological order. I wish I could have mentioned every teacher who taught here, for all have contributed to the school's strength and success.

I do not claim any literary merit, and I am not a professional historian. I have researched each profiled individual as objectively as I could, but actually this is a history of the school seen through my eyes, and as such reflects my opinions and my thoughts and the dedication and the love I feel for St. Mary's.

The material for the years 1847-1910 is gathered mainly from church and diocesan records, historical documents, newspaper articles, and school archives. Other valuable sources for me were *The Great Book* by Ellen Davies-Rodgers, *The History of St. Mary's Cathedral* by John Henry Davis, *Ten Decades of Praise* by Sister Mary Hilary, CSM, and *Sisters of St. Mary's,* author unknown. I would like to thank the Sewanee Retreat Center, especially Sister Lucy, for allowing me to make copies of letters written by the Sisters of the Order of St. Mary during their association with the school in the late 1800s. For background information on the city of Memphis, I referred to the following: *The Biography of a River Town: Its Heroic Age* by Gerald M. Capers, Jr., *Paul R. Coppock's Mid-South* by Paul R. Coppock, *Yesterday's Memphis* by Charles W. Crawford, *The Metropolis of the American Nile* by John E. Harkins, *Recollections of 92 Years* by Elizabeth Avery Meriwether 1824-1916, *Southland Writers* by Mary T. Tardy, *Cotton Row to Beale Street* by Robert A. Sigafoos, and *Elite Women and the Reform Impulse in Memphis, 1875-1915* by Marsha Wedell.

For the profiles of school leaders in later years and the present time, I have asked each one, where possible, to submit a reflection of his or her time here. I have also talked with many alumnae, faculty, staff members, and trustees for their thoughts and insights into particular individuals. My hope is that their memories, along with the many photographs, will make the school come alive. For anecdotes and thoughts from alumnae, I am indebted to the following persons: Nancy Little Oliver '45, Julia Taylor Hughes '25, Gwen Robinson Awsumb '32, Anne Howard Bailey '41, Marianne Robertson '44, Letha Cranford Elliott '54, Ann Humphreys Copp '64, Nancy Whitman Manire '64, Tish Dudley '91, Lisa Morrow Morten '76, Jeanne Stevenson Moessner '66; photography: Kathy Daniel Patterson '78; archivists: Anne Armour '73, University of the South, Ginger Hicks Cain '73, Emory University.

The following teachers and staff have been a source of constant help and encouragement: Bobbie Goforth, Angie Gardner, Ann Prince '87, Barbara Viser, Mandy Yandell, Judy Brundige, Allison Wellford Parker '83, Dianne Gregory, Pat Knight, Barbara Snyder, Kathleen McElroy, Gwenice McLaughlin, Nanette Quinn, Ann Wright, Suzanne Goza, Melissa Lofton, Julene Reed, and Sandra Pitts. In addition, I could not have written this book without the encouragement of friends and family. I am grateful to the many readers and grammarians who read and corrected the manuscript: my friends, Lois Strock, Anne Fisher, Gaye Lynn Huddleston, Mary Hills Gill, Ann Copp '64, and Sylvia Adams; my daughters, Becky Knack and Nancy Griffeth, and my sister-in-law, Nell Davis; Allison Simonton for her part in editing; Carmine Vaughan and Jean Morris (Sissy) Long for trying to keep me organized; my daughter, Sally Blood, and St. Mary's Chaplain, the Reverend Mary Katherine Allman, for encouraging me to continue; Tom Southard for the opportunity to write this history; Virginia Pretti and Kay Humphreys for support and space to work.

I am deeply indebted to all these people and many others. Without their assistance and cooperation, this book could never have been written.

— Mary M. Davis, 1997

FORWARD

In many ways, Mary Davis is St. Mary's, and the impact she has made over the past thirty-four years is remarkable. Of all the people whose lives comprise the story of St. Mary's, none has put a larger or more definitive stamp on the school than the author.

Mary Davis was destined to become an educator and to be affiliated with a school that possesses a strong and clear spiritual base. Mary's paternal great-grandfather, grandfather, and father were Presbyterian ministers, and her maternal grandfather was a college president. One uncle served as a headmaster, another became dean of a medical school, and a cousin was president of a theological seminary. Mary's parents were Presbyterian missionaries who started a school for Chinese children on the island of Hainan, just south of China's mainland, where they were serving when she was born.

After her early years in China, she returned with her family to the United States and spent her childhood in Colorado Springs, Colorado, and in Laurel, Mississippi. Immediately before her senior year in high school, her parents moved to Philadelphia, Pennsylvania, where she attended an independent girls' school, graduating at age sixteen. She earned a B.A. from Hood College in Frederick, Maryland, studied at the National College of Education in Evanston, Illinois, and later earned an M.A. from the University of Memphis.

Her exceptional education provided great assistance when tragedy struck the Davis family. Mary suffered the untimely death of her husband, David McClure Davis, who died in a tragic boating accident. Faced with supporting her family in a world in which employment for women was tenuous, Mary returned to Laurel with her children, then aged eight, six, and two.

She began her career as a secretary and bookkeeper for the Rector of St. John's Episcopal Church in Laurel and was instrumental in founding the day school that was associated with the church. Seeking broader employment opportunities, Mary moved to Memphis and became secretary and business manager at Miss Hutchison's School. The move proved fortuitous for both Mary and St. Mary's. In January of 1964, Mary hosted the Memphis Association of Independent Schools, which met at Hutchison. There, she happened to sit next to Dr. Nathaniel Hughes, the Headmaster of St. Mary's. She must have made a good impression, for in April of that year, he offered her the position of Dean of the Upper School at St. Mary's, a position she held for fifteen years. Since then, she has served as Acting Head, Alumnae Director, Development Officer, and Founding Editor of *St. Mary's News*.

Under her leadership, the Upper School—then grades seven through twelve—grew from 107 students (all housed on the third floor of the Greenwood Building) to 250 students, filling the Barth Building and the new Taylor Building. She credits the phenomenal growth and the increasing success of the school during those days to the economic growth and expansion of Memphis, to the school's connection to both the Episcopal Church and the Church of the Holy Communion, and to the school's dedication to academic excellence. These principles are perhaps best embodied in the words of Bishop Thomas Gailor, who declared in 1901, "In the long run, it pays to be honest, to be thorough, and not to pander to the popular demand for the mere social veneering which some people call 'the education of girls.'"

During this time, Mary understood that women could and should rise above the status of second-class citizen, and she continually fought for expanded horizons and opportunities for women. Radiating a rare combination of strength and warmth, Mary had the ability to build rapport with people of all ages; she developed strong and lasting relationships with students and parents, as well as with faculty and staff. Perhaps her greatest assets during her tenure as Dean were her willingness to listen and her ability to understand more than she heard—assets which continue to be two of her hallmarks.

Her seemingly easy connection to teenage girls and their complete trust in her stemmed from Mary's own experiences. The students knew absolutely that they had her ear and her heart. Because she was the much younger sister of two brothers who convinced her that (since she seemed to bear little resemblance to either parent) she was a "Chinese orphan they picked up off the street," she understood the plight of feeling that "she did not belong." Because, by her own description, she was "very tall with dark red hair and big bushy eyebrows," she understood the angst of every teenage girl whose mirror reflected less than she wished. Because her family moved a great deal, she understood the trauma that surrounded a student's moving into a new school at an awkward age. She was no stranger to hard work and self-discipline, and the students responded to her example. Indeed, by every national measure, the St. Mary's academic program and the achievement of its students proved to be extraordinary.

Mary had an equally effective relationship with the parents of her students. Herself a mother of three strong and competent women, she understood the importance of helping parents become more effective role models for their own children. And, because she was a woman of great faith, she taught by example the "calm strength and patient wisdom" necessary for helping children grow up "in an unsteady and confusing world."

For St. Mary's, Mary Davis remains a mentor and role model in the best and truest sense. Her commitment to excellence and her high expectations of us spark our willingness to reach beyond our grasp. Her acceptance of our differences allows us the freedom to become better versions of ourselves. Her faith is a shining example when our faith wavers, and her flexibility challenges us to dare. Mary's sense of humor allows us to laugh with each other and at ourselves, but above all, her wisdom and her gift of sharing it help us to become wiser.

Perhaps her greatest contribution to the school has been not in any particular role she assumed, nor in any specific task she accomplished, but in simply being who she is. St. Mary's is the school it is today in large measure because of the author of this book. Mary's spirit, vision, and guidance have helped to create the arch through which St. Mary's moves from her past to her future. We love her dearly.

— Anne Galbreath Fisher, 1997

INTRODUCTION

When I first walked into St. Mary's, I knew that it was a warm and inviting place. It had an informal atmosphere, and I immediately felt the intense interest of Headmaster Dr. N.C. Hughes, Jr. in the school and in the students and the teachers. It was obvious that his heart and mind were dedicated to St. Mary's, but his criteria for a Dean of the Upper School were so high that I knew they were impossible to reach. Later, I realized I had been right and felt I never came close to meeting them. I remember Dr. Hughes' warning, "This position demands 24 hours of one's time" and thought he was exaggerating, but I later discovered it was almost true. Because of his high expectations, Dr. Hughes' vision for the school captured my imagination and challenged me.

Never have my credentials, background, thoughts, and ideas been so thoroughly scrutinized. After at least six interviews, Dr. Hughes finally offered me the position of Dean of the Upper School. I was frightened, for I had much to learn, but delighted, for I knew this was work to which I would like to dedicate myself. This was the opportunity I had been searching for; this was the place I wanted to be.

It was not long before I felt the spirit of St. Mary's enveloping me—a spirit of excellence, personal commitment, high moral standards, and respect for each person as an individual. Guiding and sustaining this spirit through the years has been, I believe, an unwavering commitment to the spiritual life and to the Episcopal Church.

Through the years, as I have worked at St. Mary's in various positions, it has become increasingly clear to me that it is important to know the school's story intimately. I wanted to understand the reason for its existence over such a long period of time. And, in order to discover it, I went back 150 years to the autumn of 1847.

A small parish school was conceived in Calvary Episcopal Church with a woman of strong Christian faith to be its head. Ever since that year, this school has been nourished by the encouragement of the Church and by the Bishops of the Dioceses of Tennessee and West Tennessee. The school has weathered wars, epidemics, the Great Depression, and competition with other schools without losing its integrity and identity. For thirty-seven years, Sisters of the Order of St. Mary from New York taught in the school and gave strong evidence of their highest priority—commitment to the service of God. Their faith, and that of the men and women who became St. Mary's leaders, instilled a spiritual foundation which continues to be an integral part of the school today.

St. Mary's has been associated with four Episcopal churches whose Rectors have strongly supported the school: Calvary Episcopal Church, St. Mary's Cathedral, Grace-St. Luke's Episcopal Church, and, since 1953, the Church of the Holy Communion. During the past four years, St. Mary's has had her own chaplain, an ordained female Episcopal priest. The spiritual life of the students and faculty has been nourished by every one of them and by daily chapel in the sanctuary.

St. Mary's Cathedral, 1926.

The daily chapel service evokes some heartwarming memories among the alumnae. One graduate from the class of 1929 remembers clearly many prayers in the Prayer Book which were repeated each day during her six years in chapel. Although not an Episcopalian, these prayers have remained part of her memory and have supported her during hard moments in her life. Another alumna appreciated the fact that chapel was Morning Prayer—a real worship service—and not just a school assembly. She felt it would be impossible to be in chapel daily for a period of years without realizing that the world is multi-dimensional and not restricted to things that can be seen and touched. "This spiritual life is absolutely real, a habit of mind and heart that St. Mary's does not insist upon, but models persistently and passionately." One first senses its presence in the young voices of the Lower School, when they sing "Surely the Presence of the Lord is in this Place," and again when the strains of "Amazing Grace" are sung at every Senior Baccalaureate.

From modest beginnings, St. Mary's has grown from a very small school into an establishment with 800 students and approximately 150 faculty and staff. The school is known throughout the country for graduating intelligent young women of integrity who are sought by many of our nation's finest colleges. St. Mary's alumnae are renowned for their character and contributions to society. How did this occur? The story needs to be told, for it is a thrilling and poignant one. Too often we forget the power that exists in a small seed planted and nourished by faith in God and by the determination of dedicated leaders and teachers, who have had the fortitude to sacrifice and to dream. Perhaps the most important reason for the school's survival is that God has held the hands of those who have been its leaders through the years. St. Mary's has a rich story to tell.

1. THE BEGINNINGS

T he story of St. Mary's School cannot be told without first recognizing the impact on the school of the environment and events in Memphis, Tennessee, during the mid-nineteenth century. The population in Memphis was close to 1,850 when a small parish school came into existence in 1847 at Calvary Episcopal Church. Commerce in the city was dominated by flatboatmen who traveled the Mississippi River from one city to another. In 1842, a fight occurred between these flatboatmen and the Memphis Militiamen, a fight which resulted in the death of one of the flatboatmen and the forcing of the others to pay taxes. This event actually heralded the birth of Memphis as an independent city. Charles W. Crawford explains that "the control over the flatboatmen began a pattern of growth that made it one of the largest Southern cities on the eve of the Civil War."

Between this time and the 1860s, the city's population grew to 22,623 principally because of the importance of the cotton crop, the invention of the cotton gin, and its strategic location. Expanding transportation was another important factor in the development of the city: railroads joined cotton plantations and other cities to Memphis. Steamboats were a frequent sight on the Mississippi River, not only for the transportation of cotton, but also for providing "a luxurious means of travel."

Increasingly, during these years, small businesses, such as grocery stores, carriage production plants, flour mills, and machine works, appeared on the scene. Many of the wealthier citizens of Memphis built beautiful homes, some even containing ballrooms, and lavish parties were given in the Gayoso Hotel by cotton planters

Mary Foote Pope, founder 1847-1872.

moving to Memphis for the winter months. Eleven new banks made their appearance between 1853 and 1858, which revealed that Memphis was indeed prospering. The following was written by W. H. Rainey in his City Directory (1855-1856):

> The steamers on the rivers are grander than the stateliest common roads, canals are antiquated, and the railroad spirit is at its height. [Soon] we shall be within forty hours of the Atlantic Ocean … Every modern invention and improvement is brought into play, and … structures whose splendor and capacity are not exaggerated by calling them palaces are reared upon the sites of humble cabins. We are arriving at a dizzy height, but our foundations are sure.

Just as Memphis was becoming a booming metropolis, two disasters halted its growth and expansion, changing the face of the city as well as the story of St. Mary's. The first was the Civil War in the 1860s, and the second was the yellow fever outbreak in the 1870s. The story of St. Mary's comes alive against the backdrop of these circumstances because the school, along with the city, had to struggle for survival during these tumultuous years.

For many years, it was thought that St. Mary's was founded in 1869, but the surprising discovery of two artifacts by students convinced Dr. Nathaniel Cheairs Hughes, Jr. that the school was in existence before 1869. In 1965, Edie Austin, a St. Mary's student, found a book of poems in her attic authored by Mary Foote Pope, a well-known teacher and writer in the city of Memphis. On the page with the dedication, appeared the following: "St. Mary's School, Ash Wednesday, 1872." Then, at about the same time, Nell Dickerson '73 brought Dr. Hughes a medal that was given to her great-grandmother, a former St. Mary's student, by Mary Foote Pope in the year 1866.

Dr. Hughes was so intrigued by these discoveries that he assigned his history class the project of researching the life of Mary Foote Pope. Betty Abbott, Charlotte Dabbs, Janie Humphreys, Alice Cockroft, Leigh Palmer, Minna Thompson, Ann Gordon, and Martha Kittrell were among the students involved in this project.

These girls studiously searched the records of St. Mary's Cathedral and Calvary Episcopal Church as well as the morgues of *The Commercial Appeal*, the *Memphis Daily Appeal*, and *The People's Press*, a Hernando, Mississippi, newspaper. They spent time in the Memphis Public Library and visited Elmwood Cemetery. There was

The students made a little history themselves ... when they appeared at a meeting of the West Tennessee Historical Society. These girls are the first high school students ever invited to present their papers to this scholarly society. (Seated) Minna Thompson, Charlotte Dabbs, Claire McCaskill, Janie Humphreys; (standing) Betty Abbott. (The Commercial Appeal, *January 15, 1966)*

Calvary Protestant Episcopal Church, 1835-1859. Drawn by Philip W. Alston, 1843.

even an article in *The Commercial Appeal* about this effort on the part of Dr. Hughes' history class.

Their findings confirmed the fact that a small parish school was established in 1847 at Calvary Episcopal Church. Subsequent documentation made a strong statement that a connection was not only possible but probable between this parish school and St. Mary's Episcopal School.

The first mention of the existence of a parish school was found in the 1847 Vestry minutes of Calvary Episcopal Church. Dr. David Cook Page, fourth Rector of Calvary Church (1847-1854), reported the fact to the Diocesan Convention: "A Parochial School has been instituted which will greatly redound, it is trusted, to the benefit of the parish."

In July 1849, an advertisement appeared in the *Memphis Daily Eagle* presuming the possibility of the year, 1847, as the official beginning of a parish school: "Calvary Church Parochial School will commence its third term on the first Monday in August."

This discovery was of such interest to the students that they eagerly spent long hours chasing clues. Ellen Davies-Rodgers, a historian working on the history of Calvary Church, became intrigued

Besides the record in the Parish Register, the existence of this parish school was verified by letters written to Jane Eleanor (Elly) Taylor from Tiptonville, Tennessee, who became a student in this school in 1849. She lived at the home of the Reverend David Cook Page and his wife. Many letters were written to her from relatives, revealing her homesickness. Included is one from a cousin, Sarah Ann Agnes Clement, in which she was sympathetic, but urged and encouraged her to take advantage of the opportunity for a fine education. This is valuable information, for it affirms the existence of Calvary Parish School in the 1840s.

> Beaver Dam Forks, Nov 13th 1849
>
> My dear Cousin Elly
>
> I received yours of the 16th of Oct a few days past. I was very much pleased to hear from you, and hope by this time you are quite reconciled to Memphis. You said you would like to have a little fun as well as so much study. Well, Elly, as there is a time for all things under Sun, you must wait patiently until the time for fun arrives. It appears that the present is the time for study, and the improvement of those mental faculties which nature has so highly gifted you with. I think it quite natural you should love home, you have indeed a sweet home, and kind friends, who love you dearly, and think of you often, and would be so happy to hear you are contented and satisfied. I am glad you are so much pleased with Mrs Page, under the guidance of so excellent an instructress. It is your high privilege, as well as duty, to improve your time diligently in every possible way and acquire those rudiments of education which will give a tone to your character through life. You have also the invaluable privilege of attending Church often, and of being ably instructed in those inestimable truths of the Gospel, upon which rest our eternal interest. After a due consideration of so many advantages, my cousin Elly must, and will be contented, and happy as she possibly can, away from sweet home, and will no doubt offer up the tribute of her unfeigned gratitude to the Great Author of her being, for having cast her lot in such a pleasant place, and bestowing so richly upon her those unspeakable benefits which are denied so many thousands.
>
> Good-by Elly. Believe me to be, as ever, your very affectionate Cousin
>
> Sarah Ann Agnes Clement

by their findings and joined forces with the students to research the life of Mary Foote Pope. Through her findings, Mrs. Rodgers realized the possibility that this parish school could indeed be the forerunner of St. Mary's Episcopal School.

Why and when was the school named St. Mary's? There does not seem to be a definitive answer, although certain assumptions can be made. Perhaps the name was derived from Bishop Otey's interest in

The Ladies Educational and Missionary Society of Memphis have continued to prosecute the objects of their association with praise-worthy energy. They have recently secured by donation from Col. Robert Brinkley a lot suitable for the site of a small church, and have through the assistance of some friends, made a con-tract for the erection of a building ... Their enterprise affords an encouraging exam-ple of what the devotion of a few apparently weak instru-ments may by God's blessings on their persevering efforts, accomplish for the promotion of Christ's cause among us.
—Bishop Otey, 1855

education and missions which resulted in the formation of a "Ladies Educational and Missionary Society," as evidenced by his remarks to the Diocesan Convention in 1855, recorded by John H. Davis. (See sidebar.)

The Bishop's remarks reveal that this Missionary Society had a deep interest in the founding of the Mission Church on Poplar, which was built on the property referred to in the sidebar. According to John Davis:

> It has been erroneously stated that the land was donated for the church because it happened to be next to Bishop Otey's home; actually ... the church came first and the Bishop moved next door to it. The little chapel was built in 1857 and the first service to which I can find reference was on November 15, 1857. *The Daily Appeal* for November 11, refers first to the Church as the 'Mission Church on Poplar.'

An early mention of the name, St. Mary's, was in the *Diocesan Journal* of 1858: "Read prayers and preached in St. Mary's Church in Memphis, and same day baptized three children." No mention is made, however, of the priest who led the service. There is no known reference as to why or when the name was given to the Mission Church on Poplar. However, the following notice appeared in *The Daily Appeal*, November 29, 1857:

> The Mission Church on Poplar Street. This Church which has been erected by the pious zeal of the ladies belonging to the Episcopal Church of this city was organized Thanksgiving Day by the election of wardens and vestrymen. The church is called St. Mary's and the Reverend Richard Hines has been chosen Rector ...

As both the Mission Church on Poplar and Calvary Parish School were both founded by Calvary Church, it seems appropriate that they both should have the same name. Although it is not known why or for whom the name was chosen by either the Mission Church or by the school, it is known that the school was already named St. Mary's before the Foundation of the Sisters of the Order of St. Mary in New York were involved in the school. One could presume that it was named for the "Blessed Mary."

The day that St. Mary's Cathedral observes as its founding date is Ascension Day, May 13, 1858. Bishop Otey's house, built next to this church, was known as the Bishop's Home. It was during the early years of Bishop Otey's tenure as Bishop that St. Mary's Church was first called the "Bishop's Church," or Cathedral. Another connection noted between Calvary Church and St. Mary's Cathedral is that the first head of the parish school, Mrs. Le Roy Pope, is among the early communicants of St. Mary's Cathedral, becoming a member there in 1858, and returning her membership to Calvary in 1861.

There is no verified reference as to Mrs. Pope's title at Calvary Parish School. It is known, however, that Calvary Parish School was moved to another location, and that two advertisements (see sidebar) appeared in the *Memphis Daily Appeal* in 1861, both of which referred to St. Mary's School with Mrs. Pope as Principal. The first reads:

St. Mary's School, Mrs. Pope, Principal, has room for several additional boarders, that department not being at present full. The house has ample accommodations this year for 20.

The school offers to girls every advantage for thorough mental training and elegant accomplishments that northern institutions can give. The limited number enables the principal to be personally cognizant of the progress of each pupil, and all the assistants have been long connected with the School. Mr. Winkler continues, as in years past, to control the Music. (*Memphis Daily Appeal*, January 1, 1861)

Mrs. Pope's husband, Le Roy Pope, became Superintendent of the Public Schools in Memphis in 1857, and was also trustee of the Memphis Medical College, demonstrating that they both had a vital interest in education.

Imagine their provocative and lively conversations on the subject. In *Biographical Notices of Graduates of Yale College* by F.B. Dexter, there is this notice about Mr. Pope which includes mention of his wife, Mary:

He was a member of the Episcopal Church and while living in Memphis was largely instrumental in the establishment of Calvary Church, of which he was a vestryman. His wife was the founder and President of St. Mary's Episcopal Institute in Memphis, a boarding school for girls.

Although Mary and Le Roy Pope had four children, her mother lived with them freeing Mary to teach, a role for which she was eminently qualified because of her educational background.

Mary Pope was tutored in a private school in Huntsville, Alabama, and was exposed to a strong academic education,

One of the poems printed in Poems *reflects Mrs. Pope's optimistic and joyous attitude towards life:*

THE GIFT OF SONG
If, when bright visions o'er
thee throng,
They clothe themselves in
words of song,
And strengthen and refresh
thy soul;
Though weak and faint
the numbers roll
Yet fear not thou to sing,
If common life to thee
keep tune
Unto thy spirit's
chaunting rune
And all the actual
grows bright
Neath fancy's soft
ideal light,
Thou has the power
to sing.

becoming proficient in Latin, Greek, German, and mathematics, amazing for a woman of her generation. A lover of poetry and writing, she published several books of poetry and some of her poems appeared in periodicals of that day. These revealed her thoughts about the war, about her four children, and about her philosophy of life. A copy of one of her books now resides in the St. Mary's School Archives. It is entitled *Poems* and was published by J. B. Lippincott & Co., in 1872.

A crystal-clear portrait of Mary Foote Pope is given in *Southland Writers* by Mary T. Tardy:

> As a young lady, Miss Foote possessed a beautiful, dreamy face, and her form of aerial grace personified the ideal of poesy … Her life has been chequered by misfortune and sorrow, which have only seemed to give occasion for the development of the lofty and noble qualities of her nature. Mrs. Pope is the mother of Lieutenant W.S. Pope, killed at Tishomingo Creek, and mentioned in the life of General Bedford Forrest. Mrs. Pope has grappled with adversity with a bold, unqualing spirit, and ridden triumphant over the storms of life. She has charge of a flourishing school for young ladies in Memphis, which sufficiently attests the indomitable energy dwelling in her slender and fragile figure. The sweet murmurings of her muse may be frequently heard floating on the breeze, in the Memphis journals.

As Dr. Hughes' students delved more deeply into Mary Pope's background, they discovered that she was not only a woman with twentieth century characteristics, but also a woman determined and loyal to the causes in which she believed, particularly education and the Confederacy. She also was a devotee of States Rights and proposed an organization of women in the South called "The Southern Mothers." The following article from the *Memphis Daily Appeal* (March 21, 1861), is a persuasive one, filled with passionate pleading for the support of these sons of the South and her encouragement of the mothers to give aid to the wounded soldiers of the Confederate Army:

> To the Mothers of the South—
> While the men in every part of the country are arousing themselves and mustering in squadrons to resist the invasion and oppression threatening our beloved land, let us emulate the enthusiasm of our husbands, sons and friends in the cause. Many of our daughters are already active in the

service with their needles. Let the matrons of every city, village and hamlet form themselves into societies called by some appropriate name, pledged to take care of the sick and wounded soldiers of the Confederate army … Let the women of the entire South join and spread the organization till not a spot within the southern borders shall be without a band of sisters pledged to the work and ready for it; and thus shall every mother be assured in sending her son to the field, that in time of need they shall have the tender care of some other mother whose loved ones are in the patriot ranks at other points; and our soldiers feel sure that true hearts are near them, wherever they may be.

The Union soldiers occupied Memphis on June 6, 1862. Fortunately Memphis escaped some of the destruction many other southern towns experienced, but, according to Gerald M. Capers, Jr., "until the end of the hostilities, it was continually within a short distance of irregular operations." Although Memphis was now held by the Union, Mrs. Pope continued to fly the Confederate flag in defiance of an order by a federal officer. Despite the fact that she was threatened with banishment, she would not change her loyalties nor would she desert her school. Like Mrs. Meriwether, author and loyal Rebel supporter, she was banished from the City of Memphis and in 1862 moved the school to Hernando, Mississippi. This defiance and demonstration of initiative on her part gives a glimpse of an enterprising woman loyal to her principles regardless of the consequences. Her great-grandson underscored this trait by reaffirming this opinion of her: "She was strengthened in character by adversity." Being a person of great loyalty, there is no doubt that she continued to fly the Confederate flag with pride in front of her school in Hernando.

An autobiographical book by Elizabeth Avery Meriwether entitled *Recollections of 92 Years, 1824-1916*, published by the Tennessee Historical Society in 1958, dramatically reveals the perilous situation in Memphis and the danger for the rebel wives during the time Mrs. Pope was head of St. Mary's School. In this book, Mrs. Meriwether relates a conversation with General Sherman asking him for assistance to leave Memphis with her two small sons. His reply was to banish her because she "allowed" her husband to be in the Rebel Army. The following order was given by him: "He would banish ten rebel families from Memphis for every one of his Gun Boats fired on by the Confederates." Mrs. Meriwether was one of ten wives forced to leave Memphis in one day or be placed in the Irving

Block, an office building on Second Street that had been turned into a prison by General Sherman. This was the same year Mary Pope was banished from the city of Memphis for flying the Confederate Flag. A note written by Lee Meriwether, her son, in May 1958 affirms General Sherman's statement: "I am not interested in rebel wives or rebel brats; if you are in Memphis day after tomorrow you will be imprisoned for the duration of the rebellion." Mrs. Meriwether left Memphis eight-months pregnant with two children under the age of five on a wagon pulled by "a member of the family, Adrienne," her mule. And so she began her pilgrimage into Mississippi.

An understanding of the condition of the roads between Memphis and Hernando is given in Mrs. Meriwether's book:

> The roads were very bad, not having been worked since the beginning of the war, and I feared every minute a wheel would slide into a gully or get knocked off on a rock or a roof and then that we would all be overturned and perhaps killed … We jogged along very slowly between wasted fields and through lonely forests, for a long time seeing not a human being. The farm houses in that region were deserted … a lonely lane between two fields with broken down fences.

In this description of the countryside in 1862, Mrs. Meriwether gives a clear picture of the roads as they must have been when Mary Pope was traveling these same roads to and from Hernando, a bleak picture revealing the determination and bravery of Mrs. Pope and women like her during the Civil War. Although Mrs. Pope was not a rebel wife, her two sons were in the Rebel army, and one was killed. In *The Military Annals of Tennessee*, June 10, 1864, is this eulogy:

> Here, too, was killed the lamented and gallant adjutant William S. Pope, an officer greatly beloved in the regiment and who had eminently distinguished himself on the field of daring bravery.

As Mrs. Pope traveled these muddy, bumpy, treacherous roads to Hernando, were the Union soldiers surrounding and taunting her about her strategy to move the school to Hernando? How did the students manage to attend school, considering the difficulties of transportation? Were there both day and boarding students? What did she do for equipment and supplies? Surely, given the condition of the countryside, most of her students must have been boarding students or residents of Hernando.

The road [between Hernando and Memphis] was desolate and dreary; the farm houses on either side of the road were either in ashes or abandoned by their owners. We saw no animals on the way, not a horse or cow or sheep—silence reigned everywhere.

—Elizabeth Avery Meriwether, 1863

Gwyn Place, first home of St. Mary's in Hernando, Mississippi (renovated).

Wondering about Mrs. Pope's courageous move from Memphis influenced me to visit Hernando to verify the above information about the school's existence there. My visit proved to be worthwhile for I saw Gwyn Place where the school was originally held. It has been renovated and is now a home.

I discovered a picture of the Baptist Female College which is no longer in existence. I also found advertisements in *The People's Press*

Baptist Female College, the second home of St. Mary's in Hernando, 1862.

about Mrs. Pope's School. This experience made St. Mary's existence in Hernando come alive for me.

Existing records give proof that the school was moved in 1862 to a Presbyterian Church in Hernando known as Gwyn Place and in 1865 to the Baptist Female College. There are also two artifacts from this period of the school's history: the medal, previously mentioned, awarded to a graduate and a school newspaper called *The Bouquet*.

The Bouquet, *January 1, 1866, student newspaper.*

The Bouquet was the brain-child of Miss Lem Cooke and Miss Fanny Boon while they were attending St. Mary's in Hernando. The printer is even known; it was Ledger Steam Book and Job Printing Office, 143 Madison Street, Memphis.

A copy of the January 1, 1866, issue of *The Bouquet* was discovered almost exactly one hundred years later in the Hernando Library by Dr. Hughes' students. Since then, it has been stored in the Genealogical Room at the Court House in Hernando. This issue included a notice about the school and several other advertisements, demonstrating that although the times have changed, the youth of every age delight in being creative and witty.

> **WANTED:** Someone to help me to search for my sense; but there is so little of it, wherever it may be, that none need apply but those gifted with remarkably keen observation.

> **FOUND:** A poor little slate pencil, which has been long wandering about the school room floor in a very destitute condition. The owner after eating on it for a long time, threw it away. We hope she will be benevolent enough to come forward and claim and provide for the superannuated servant, who can be found by calling at desk No. 1, first row.

> **LOST:** A Thirty, almost in the grasp of one of the young ladies in the Mental Arithmetic class, which it is feared will never be found, as it has been washed away by her tears and carried to that land from whose bourne no thirties ever retain, and entombed by a stroke of the Principal's pencil. 'There's many a slip between the lip and the cup.'

From March 8 to June 14, 1866, there were almost weekly advertisements in the Hernando newspaper in which Mary Pope glowingly pictures life at St. Mary's. In the following statement, Mrs. Pope gives an enthusiastic description of her school along with its curriculum. She demonstrates an expert knack for clarifying the mission of the school in meticulous, concise words.

> Mrs. Pope's School commenced the sixth session in Hernando, Miss., and the twentieth since its opening in Memphis, Tennessee, February 1, in the Baptist Female College. No pains are spared by the Principal to render the course of study complete, and the instruction thorough in every department; and she never had more efficient assistance than now. Circulars containing terms furnished at the school. Persons having business with teachers or pupils are requested, if possible, to call after 3 P.M. Books and stationery can be obtained at the school at Memphis prices, for cash. (*The People's Press*)

FEMALE COLLEGE!

MRS. POPE,

WILL commence the seventh Session of her School in Hernando, the

First of September.

No pains will be spared to maintain the high character of the school. The number will be limited.

☞ MRS. POPE earnestly begs all indebted to her to make immediate settlement, as she desires as soon as possible after the close of the session, to remove the remains of her son Adjutant POPE, from the battle-field near Tishimingo creek, to Memphis, and needs the money due her, for that purpose.

June 21, 1866-tf.

A pointed but poignant advertisement appeared in The People's Press *on June 21, 1866.*

ST. MARY'S SCHOOL
FOR GIRLS.

Poplar Street, East of Orleans Street.

MEMPHIS, - - - - - TENNESSEE.

A School of the Protestant Episcopal Church,

OFFERING THE VERY BEST ADVANTAGES
In all branches of Education.

MARY E. POPE, Principal.

This advertisement discloses the fact that the location of St. Mary's was again on Poplar Street, adjacent to St. Mary's Cathedral. This information makes a strong statement that St. Mary's School was an Episcopal school.

Evidence from two letters reveal that Mrs. Pope continued to run the school until 1872. A copy of a letter written by Jefferson Davis to Mrs. M.E. Pope verifies that he was invited to the school on the occasion of the Bishop's lecture. Le Roy Pope, her grandson, wrote a letter indicating an association between Mary Pope and Bishop Quintard:

I am afraid I cannot tell you too much about St. Mary's School except that it was founded by my great grandmother, Mary Elizabeth Foote Pope. Bishop Quintard gave her assistance.

The very definite statement that this was the *twentieth* year of the school's operation documents again the fact that this school had been in existence since 1847 under the same principal, although originally under a different name.

St. Mary's School first reappeared on Poplar Street in Memphis in 1868. There are no detailed accounts of this move, but this return to Memphis is documented in advertisements. One reveals that the school was no longer occupying space at the Baptist College in Hernando as the College was trying to lease its property:

1868. Board agrees to rent the Baptist College Building to anyone.

When Mrs. Pope moved the school back to Memphis in 1868, she occupied the building at 350 Poplar owned by Dr. Hines, which was his residence and also had been known as "Dr. Hines School."

Memphis Tn
9th May 1870

Mrs. M. E. Pope
Dear Madam,

accept my thanks for your kind consideration in inviting me to meet your School and friends on the occasion of the Bishop's lecture, last Saturday evening.

The invitation did not reach me until Sunday morning.

With sincere regard I am very respectfully yours,

Jefferson Davis

Very little is documented about Mary Pope after 1873, when the Sisters were appointed to be in charge of the school, until the time of her death in 1905. It is known that she taught in public schools and that she tutored pupils privately, for one of her students was Charlotte Gailor, daughter of Bishop Gailor, who followed Bishop Quintard as Bishop of Tennessee. Two notices indicate that Mary Pope was no longer with the school late in 1872 and that the school was under the direction of Bishop Quintard by 1873:

> St. Mary's School for Young Ladies, 350 Poplar. St. Mary's School under the supervision of the Rt. Rev. (Bp.) C.T. Quintard offers to parents and guardians every advantage of a thorough and liberal education for young ladies. Session opens September 10. For further particulars apply to Mr. Leonard Sewell, Principal.

> L. Sewell, Principal St. Mary's school, 350 Poplar. Ward 8 (3 males, 12 females).

Mary Pope died in 1905. She lived the last years of her life in the Mary Galloway Home. Her funeral service was held at the home of Felix Pope, a nephew, and the funeral address was delivered by Dr. F.P. Davenport, Rector of Calvary Episcopal Church where she had been a member for three quarters of a century, except for the brief time she had been a member of St. Mary's Cathedral. Her burial at Elmwood Cemetery was attended by many of her former pupils. In a

Blessing of Mary Pope's tombstone by Bishop James M. Coleman with Mary Pope's descendant, Piper Gray, St. Mary's student, class of 2004.

Mary Pope's tombstone reads:

Mary Foote Pope
1821-1905
Place at my head, of gray
stone wrought,
A cross, that to the
passing eye
May tell — oh, sweet and
blessed thought!
That Christian ashes
'neath it lie.

Mary Foote Pope
Poet and Founder of
St. Mary's Episcopal School
Memphis, Tennessee 1847

notice of her death published in *The Commercial Appeal*, it was suggested that "all her former pupils attend the funeral ceremony wearing a white carnation."

Although Mary Foote Pope was buried in Elmwood Cemetery, it was not until 1998 that her grave was marked with a tombstone. In a beautiful ceremony at Elmwood, this tombstone was given in her honor by the class of 1997 and by the former and present headmasters of the school. St. Mary's felt it was not only appropriate but necessary that the founder of this fine school have a marker for her grave. St. Mary's cherishes the knowledge that a woman believing in women's potential to achieve greatness had the foresight to open the school and also the dogged determination to keep it alive. Based on research conducted over the past thirty years, it appears believable and probable that Calvary Parish School, later named St. Mary's and then St. Mary's Episcopal School, is the forerunner of the present St. Mary's Episcopal School.

2. DEVOTION AND DEDICATION

I n 1873, Sisters of the Order of St. Mary in New York arrived in Memphis to teach, but also accepted with grace the immediate need to serve the community. I have been touched and brought to tears by the many letters written by these Sisters to the Mother House in New York who described their experiences during the yellow fever epidemics.

As I read and re-read these letters, I discover their story, but primarily I am given a beautiful picture of God's love. It seems evident that the timing of their arrival in Memphis was providential for both the city and the school.

Following the Civil War, women, in addition to church and volunteer work, became more interested and involved in the civic and community life of Memphis. Elizabeth Meriwether was an early advocate of "Women's Rights," involving herself through newspaper articles and at public rallies in their right to vote. According to Robert A. Sigafoos, she "organized the Tennessee Equal Rights Association to fight equality rights for both men and women." Furthermore, Mrs. Meriwether was the first woman in the South to speak and write about woman's suffrage. In John E. Harkin's account, she even "forced herself into the polls and voted in the 1870s. She suspected that her ballot was never counted, but it gave her a claim to being the first woman to vote in U.S. elections."

During these years, another concern of women was the educational system in Memphis. Marsha Wedell notes the progression of women's education:

Charles Todd Quintard, Second Bishop of Tennessee. The importance of Bishop Quintard in the annals of St. Mary's School cannot be over-emphasized, for it was his idea to engage the Sisters to teach in the school.

Clara Conway, one of the city's respected educators, was nominated unsuccessfully for the position of superintendent of public schools ... [and that] she and Jenny Higbee (an Easterner who moved to Memphis) ... provided an important bridge to the larger female world and ... exercised great influence upon a developing women's culture.

Both of these women opened their own school for girls in the 1870s, hoping to "prepare graduates for the entrance into the best women's colleges." St. Mary's, already in existence, continued to emphasize this same thread of academic excellence by preparing students for admission to fine colleges.

St. Mary's story during the 1870s is an unbelievable one of sacrifice, service, and survival. This chapter of the life of the school began under the leadership of the Right Reverend Quintard, Bishop of the Diocese of Tennessee. Sister Mary Hilary describes him as a New Englander, "a descendant of a Huguenot family, black-eyed, magnetic, buoyant and direct." He received his medical degree from the University Medical College in New York (later NYU) in 1847 and practiced medicine for four years in Athens, Georgia, moving to Memphis in 1851 to be professor of physiology and pathological anatomy at the Memphis Medical College. His close friendship with the Right Reverend James Hervey Otey, first Bishop of Tennessee, 1834-1863, influenced him to become a candidate for the Holy Orders. He worked for a short time in Tipton County and in 1856 was called to be Rector of Calvary Episcopal Church in Memphis. Although he stayed there only a year, it was an important time, for during this year, as John H. Davis explains, "Calvary's second mission church—St. Mary's—was founded in order to reach the inhabitants of the suburbs of East Memphis."

During his New England days, Bishop Quintard had become close friends with Mother Harriet of the Order of St. Mary in New York and was eager to have a branch of the sisterhood in Memphis to assist in establishing a newly created Church Home and to teach in St. Mary's School. Mother Harriet was a gracious, intelligent, and dedicated person who had been associated with The House of Mercy, St. Luke's Hospital, and St. Mary's School in New York City. A description of her during her late teenage years does not predict her future accurately, for Harriet was described as being "a great society girl and not at all religious." She played both the piano and organ, and her plan was to move to California to live with her sister and to

The Foundation also bought property in Peekskill, New York, in 1872, where they opened St. Gabriel's School, but they were in such financial straits that they did not have enough money to pay twenty-five cents for a C.O.D. package. Nor were the Sisters welcomed with any enthusiasm at a nearby St. Peter's Church, for in their black habits they were looked upon with suspicion. They were assigned a pew, but there were too many sisters to fit into one pew, and one of the Sisters had to put her feet into the aisle. Finally, the vestry heard their pleas for more room and placed a hinged board on the outside of the front pew. Later, Sister Mary Hilary related that during the sermon "the hinges gave way and to their surprise and dismay, the Sisters fell to the floor."

teach music, but a short time before she had expected to leave, her sister died. As a result, Harriet remained in New York and was so inspired by the Sisterhood that she became a probationer in the Sisterhood of the Holy Communion. Her responsibility was to nurse and to care for extremely ill patients. In 1865, she was accepted into the Sisterhood of St. Mary in New York and later was elected Sister Superior. St. Mary's School moved to 60 East 46th Street in New York City in 1871, and was noted for its high academic standards. To verify this, "the salutatory" at graduation was delivered in French and was followed by sixteen essays and recitations in Latin, German, and English.

In 1867, Bishop Quintard organized a home for Civil War orphans and asked Mother Harriet for assistance. With the help of the Churchmen of Tennessee, he was able to raise $14,000 for this home for orphans, a remarkable amount of money for that time. The donation and the gift of land in Buntyn made it possible to construct this building. A young woman, clothed as Minor Sister Martha from Nashville, was sent to New York to be trained by Mother Harriet to work in the orphanage, but within a few months, there was urgent need for her to come to Memphis to manage the home. She worked at the home in Memphis for approximately a year and a half, returning to the Mother House for further training. Unfortunately, she became ill while in the East and died at the House of Mercy in New York.

According to Sister Mary Hilary, after continual urging from Bishop Quintard, and with the consent of the Bishop of New York, Mother Harriet finally agreed to open a Foundation in Memphis in 1872. This Foundation would include the School and the Orphanage. Before she made a decision, however, she requested the Bishop to give her the answer to several questions:

> Shall we have the privilege of daily celebration? Can the Sisters look upon you as their spiritual guide? As to temporal affairs, we have no money. Can the house be secured to us free of rent for one or more years? Will any gentleman or gentlemen hold themselves responsible to make up any deficiency in our current expenses for one or more years? The School should be a Boarding and Day school. Will a strong effort be made to secure pupils from all parts of the Diocese?

The response to these requests was favorable, for in May 1873, Sister Constance was appointed by Mother Harriet to be Sister Superior of this new Foundation in the South. She was only

Sister Constance, Sister Superior.
St. Mary's Episcopal School,
1873-1878.

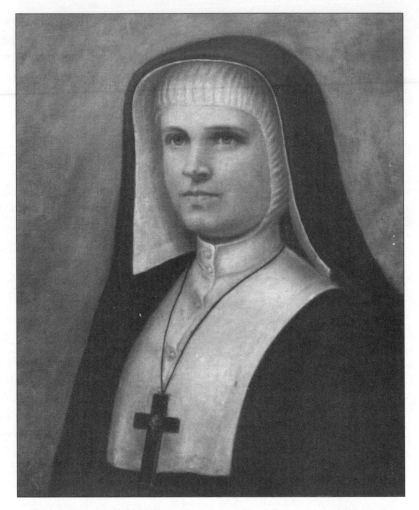

twenty-eight years old, but "she was a talented artist, an able teacher and linguist, and possessed of charm which 'might have adorned the most brilliant social circle.'" Originally a Unitarian, she braved her family's indignation to become a Christian. Three Sisters accompanied Sister Constance to Memphis, Sister Thecla and Sister Hughetta to work at the school with her, and Sister Amelia to be Director of the Church Home.

Later in the year, Bishop Quintard moved to Sewanee, making the Bishop's home west of the Cathedral available for the school. For a short time, the Sisters lived at the home of Sister Hughetta's brother, Colonel Robert Snowden, and during this period, began renovating the Bishop's home to make it suitable for a school. Their total assets of $235 came from one of the Sisters selling her watch

Sister Hughetta, Sister Superior, St. Mary's Episcopal School, 1878-1902.

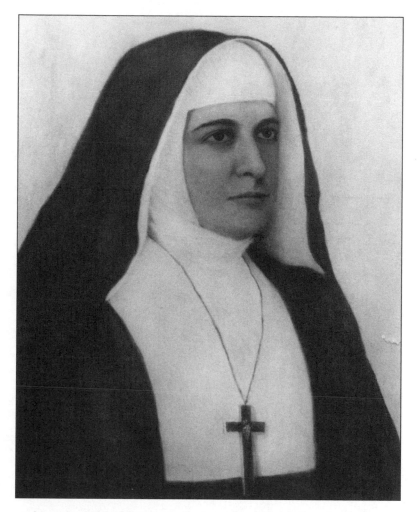

and jewelry. With this money, they purchased a chalice for $125 which left only the meager sum of $110 to open the school. By this sacrificial act, they quickly demonstrated their first priority—dedication to the spiritual life. This chalice was a part of their daily chapel service at the school and is still used by the Sisters in Sewanee who graciously allowed St. Mary's School to use it for a special service in 1996. The chalice is a symbol of constancy, faith, self-sacrifice, care, compassion, and hope.

The earliest brochure for St. Mary's School that I could find was printed the 1873-74 school year. The school was run in similar fashion to the New York Schools of the Order of St. Mary. There were four departments: Kindergarten, Primary, Grammar School, and Academic; the requirements for graduation were English,

St. Mary's School brochure, 1873.

1873—1898.

S. MARY'S SCHOOL,

FOR GIRLS.

UNDER THE CHARGE OF THE

SISTERS OF S. MARY OF THE EPISCOPAL CHURCH,

364-366 POPLAR STREET,

MEMPHIS, TENN.

REFERENCES.

Reference is made to the following patrons of the School:

BISHOP T. F. GAILOR,	PINCKNEY LATHAM,
R. B SNOWDEN,	J. J. FREEMAN,
GEORGE ARNOLD,	H. W. JAMES,
T. B EDGINGTON,	ROBT. COOPER,
J. BLINKLEY,	F. M. NILES,
J. ROBINSON,	E. M. ESTES,
A. I. ELCAN, M.D.	GEORGE JAMES,
ROLT. JONES,	H. C. HOSKINS,
J. PROUDFIT.	

The following curriculum was for the senior class:

• Rhetoric—Versification, Prose Composition
• Literature—Nineteenth-Century Authors' Study of Chaucer
• Science—Chemistry, with Laboratory work
• Trigonometry
• History—Constitutional History of England, first half of year, Constitutional History of America, second half of the year
• Latin, Virgil, The Aeneid *and* Ecologues, *Grammar, Latin Prose and Composition*
• Greek—Homer's Iliad, *Greek Prose Composition*
• Physical Culture
• Psychology

A detailed account of the curriculum in French and German is given. Also, there were electives: Elocution— One Hundred and Eighty Emotional Studies; Music— vocal and piano; Art— watercolors, crayons, and painting on china.

Mathematics, Science, and Classics. A student who earned the grade of ninety in reports and examinations was on the Roll of Honor. After three years on the Roll of Honor, the student received St. Mary's Gold Medal.

Other instructors besides the Sisters were the Reverend William Klein, a professor at the University of the South, later Dean of St. Mary's Cathedral, who taught higher mathematics, Latin, and German, Mme. Harriet Delamare from Paris who taught French and vocal music, and Miss Lewin who taught natural science. Trips and vacations for students were even offered in those days, mainly, it seems, for health reasons. Students who were in need of a change of

The expenses per half-year as found in the 1873 brochure.

EXPENSES PER HALF YEAR.

DAY PUPILS.

Tuition in Academic Department	$ 28.00
Tuition in Grammar School	25.00
Tuition in Primary School	20.00
Class Lessons in Elocution	10.00
Private Lessons in Elocution	25.00
Lessons in Oil Painting	25.00
Lessons in Water Colors	20.00
Lessons in Drawing	20.00
Embroidery	15.00
French	20.00
German	20.00
Private Lessons in Vocal Music	40.00
Class Lessons in Vocal Music	10.00
Lessons in Instrumental Music, Piano, Violin or Organ	40.00
Guitar, Banjo or Mandolin	30.00
Use of Piano	10.00
Latin, Greek, Calisthenics, Physical Culture, no extra charge.	
Graduation Fee	10.00
Library Fee	1.00

BOARDING PUPILS.

Boarding, per half year	$100.00
Tuition, according to class.	
Laundry Expenses	10.00

LIBRARY.

S. Mary's possesses a very good Library. A large and beautiful room has been fitted to receive the many valuable books that have been given to the school.

10

A sentence near the end of this brochure gives a convincing reason for the school's future success:

The Sisters did not measure their success by the extent, but the thoroughness of their work. They rather look forward to the gradual development of a high-toned system of education, than rest in what has been accomplished.

air would be taken to S. Mary's on the Mountain, Sewanee, or the Highlands of New York. The financial terms were six dollars per week.

The Sisters' plan was to open the school on October 1, 1873, to boarding and day students. Unfortunately, their hopes were dashed, for that day was the beginning of a major yellow fever outbreak. The condition of the city of Memphis was deplorable at this time. There was no adequate sanitation system and there were many defective cisterns and wells. By one account, the streets were "huge depots of filth." It was an extremely dangerous period for the Sisters to arrive in Memphis, for there had been several epidemics preceding their arrival. There was an "Epizootic" epidemic, an equine disease that

Bishop Quintard and Dean Harris of the Cathedral gave many glowing reports of the heroism and dedication of the Sisters:

> *They devoted themselves night and day to visiting the sick and afflicted, kneeling at the bedside in prayer, ministering as nurses, braving the pestilential air, and going from house to house and from hovel to hovel serving the Lord Christ in His poor and afflicted ones.*

paralyzed all the horse drawn traffic in Memphis. This was followed by a virulent form of smallpox, a mild form of cholera, and the yellow fever epidemic. That year, there was even a deep freeze to add to their problems.

Five thousand people were stricken with yellow fever in the city. A Catholic priest urged the Sisters to nurse the victims, but upon discovering they were teachers and not nurses, the priest refused to allow them to endanger their lives. They quickly became involved, however, as the city was divided into separate nursing districts. These sisters became responsible for the Cathedral District.

Sister Mary Hilary explains that at that time no one knew that mosquitoes carried the disease; the thought was that the pestilence was due to the night air, and to clean the air, they used carbolic acid in the streets and homes.

Except for tea and vespers, which they never missed, these Sisters worked from early morning until late at night. Naturally, they became exhausted. Sister Constance wrote long letters to Mother Harriet in New York revealing her feelings:

> A pouring rain ... just stirs up the horrible filth of this wretched city, and leaves muddy pools to stagnate in the sun. There is no drainage—no system of cleaning the city— everyone carries the kitchen refuse into the back alley, and the pigs, which run about the streets, eat it up. I have disinfected this house thoroughly, from garret to cellar, with lime, carbolic acid, and copperas, and today the health officer came and threw tar-water all about the place— spoiling our nice clean galleries and spotting the hall carpeting in the most unnecessary manner.

As I picture these women in their daily round of duties, I wonder if the word, "Saints," instead of "Sisters," would not paint a more accurate portrait.

Following this epidemic, the school opened in November 1873, albeit with only four students. Enrollment increased to twenty by the end of December, and to forty by the end of the school year. The increase in enrollment was so encouraging that the Sisters decided to purchase property east of the Cathedral for $7,000, which they borrowed from Robert Brinkley.

A year later, in the fall of 1874, the school doubled its enrollment and actually opened with 80 students. By 1875, the enrollment had increased to 100.

Students attending St. Mary's in the 1870s.

The Sisters' total life was dedicated to the operation of the school. Sister Constance became Sister Superior, keeping accounts, supervising each of the associates, and managing the academic department, as well as teaching Latin, French, and history. Sister Thecla, the sacristan of both the Cathedral and the school chapel, oversaw the music department, instructed piano, managed the primary school, and taught English and Latin grammar. Neither her Saturdays nor Sundays were days of rest, for she was busy visiting the poor and sick on these days. Sister Hughetta's responsibilities consisted of teaching art, mathematics, and English composition. She was also in charge of the house and supervised the Guild of the Holy Child, a devotional society for school girls founded by Mother Harriet. One of Sister Hughetta's comments during these years was that "they lived in a flow of charity and prayers that made life very sweet and all burdens light." It was, however, a difficult life, for during winter mornings, they would often find their water frozen in their pitchers. Summers were worse because of the stench and filth of the city. Sister Mary Hilary believed their dedication to work was softened by the knowledge that "St. Mary's was probably the best church school in the southern states at that time."

The Church Home, directed by Sister Amelia, was also a busy place because of the many children who were left orphans by the yellow fever epidemic. Unfortunately, Sister Amelia had to resign her position, and it was not until 1877 that a replacement could be found. At that time, Mother Harriet appointed Sister Frances to be its Director.

Commencement was a special time at St. Mary's, greatly anticipated by the seniors. Hand-illuminated diplomas designed and made by the Sister Superior were given to the graduates. These were presented by Bishop Quintard, and later by Bishop Gailor, who both delighted in being a part of the ceremony and giving the blessing. The ceremony was followed by a social hour picturesquely described by Sister Mary Hilary:

> Scores of white-gowned girls with huge bouquets of flowers and scores of little girls running about with the flower baskets of the seniors; of dignified fathers and happy mothers smiling upon their children, while in and out of the crowded rooms moved the stately ... waiters carrying ice cream and cake on large silver trays being the property of rich and kindly neighbors.

It was the custom to award a gold cross to the valedictorian. One of St. Mary's present teachers, Mary Hills Divine Gill, proudly wears the gold cross which was given to her grandmother, Elinor Sellers, in 1892 for being valedictorian. Above, both sides of the gold cross are shown.

Lizzie Montgomery's valedictory address given at commencement in 1876 is an excellent example of a "perfect period piece of commencement oratory." Valedictory addresses are still given at each commencement at St. Mary's, but they differ considerably from the ones of the late 19th century. Language then was more flowery and sentimental as demonstrated by the last paragraph of Lizzie Montgomery's address:

> Schoolmates—Farewell! I fain would not have it so. What words can express my feelings for you. If the poet can say so much of the frail, soulless flowers of our parterres and fields, what does he leave me to say to you, my beautiful flowers, with germs of eternity in each heart? There is nothing more to say. To you whom in this rose-bud garden

of girls I have likened unto flowers rich, rare, sweet flowers-
done so pure and fair I have named a lily, another the
goddess of Flowers herself, and one in all her youthful
beauty a rose, another a modest daisy, others violets and
heliotropes, pinks, and pansies all buds, and blossoms—
may your lives be as gentle and lovely as these flowers; may
no dark shadows, no heavy storms impend your pathway,
so that when death comes to call from each circle its fondly
cherished one, angels may bear that soul to its God.

To the discouragement and sorrow of everyone, there was
another yellow fever epidemic beginning in the summer of 1878,
which was even more violent and fatal than the one in 1873, causing
panic among the people in Memphis.

The following is written by an anonymous author who described
Memphis at that time:

Thousands left on trains, whilst thousands of others
escaped in carriages, wagons, carts, and even on foot … On
any road leading out of Memphis, could be seen a proces-
sion of wagons, piled high with beds, trunks, and small
furniture, carrying, also, the women and children … The
scenes at the depots were wild and exciting to the highest
degree. A friend wrote back from Louisville, 'We were
unable to get standing room on the trains on Wednesday
and Thursday, but we left on Friday … The scene I wit-
nessed at the depot could not be pictured … At last the
over-crowded train moved off amid the loud and heart-
rending cries of those left behind. I was told that a child and
an old person were trampled to death near us on the plat-
form.' By the middle of the following week all who desired
to escape and had the means of doing so were gone, and
the city was still and death-like. There was something wonderfully moving to the soul in this contrast—this change
from wild and terrible confusion to the calm stillness of the
deserted streets, the closed stores and houses, the rapid
passing of hearses and wagons with the dead.

At the beginning of this second epidemic, Sisters Constance and
Thecla were vacationing at St. Gabriel's School in Peekskill, New
York. As soon as they heard about the new outbreak, they left immediately for Memphis to once again nurse the yellow fever victims.
They made a brief stopover at Trinity Infirmary in New York to
arrange for money and supplies to be sent to Memphis. The Sunday
following their departure, the Reverend George H. Houghton, Rector

of the Church of Transfiguration in New York, made these remarks about the Sisters to the congregation:

> Without delay or hesitation they went back to the post of duty and of danger, and, it may be, of death. I have had a varied experience, and have witnessed much, but I have seen no braver sight than that which I saw in front of the Trinity Infirmary, when, just at evening, I blessed those sisters sitting alone in the carriage which was to take them to Memphis. Is it much for us who are to come, please God, into no such peril of death, to fill their hands with such things as they need for the sick and the dying and the destitute? Upon their arrival in Memphis, there was the initial suggestion they work in the city in the daytime and sleep in the country at night. This they turned down immediately with the reply, 'We are going to nurse day and night; we must be at our post.'

St. Mary's School had to be closed again and was turned into a dispensary. One is awed by the setbacks, one after another, endured by the Sisters, and inspired by their devotion and dedication to the yellow fever victims. The Sisters also were in charge of the Church Home, and their responsibilities were increased by the Relief Association's request to take over the Canfield Asylum. This Asylum was a home for Negro children started by Martha Canfield in the 1860s and was under the sponsorship of the Cathedral. As the disease became more and more widespread, it was necessary for the city to devise a plan for taking care of the orphans. The Relief Association decided this orphanage would become a place for all orphans "without any distinction as to race or religion." The Sisters agreed to be in charge. The Asylum was located in a place they felt was safe from the disease, although actually, there was no such place. A vivid picture of the situation in Memphis is as follows:

> The Relief Association appealed to the sisters to receive the children being now daily left orphans by the fever. It was furnished and mainly supported by the Relief Association … The opening (of the asylum) was attended by unpleasant circumstances. On our way to the Asylum we were met by a mob of men, who stopped our carriage and protested against the children being brought from the infected districts to their neighborhood. One man said, 'I have brought my wife and children here from the lower parts of the city to save them from the fever, and I won't have these orphans brought out here.' And the leader flourished a roll of paper

Deaths averaged ten a day, and the city was panicked. During 1878, 35,000 left Memphis in fear of the epidemic, leaving about 20,000 in the city. There was still no scientific knowledge of the cause of yellow fever; it was still believed to be transmitted through the atmosphere. The number of victims kept increasing and the Board of Health was at a loss about the action it needed to take. Sister Mary Hilary reported that the Board did vote on August 29, "to prohibit the importation of watermelons and ordered that fever victims be coffined and buried within six hours of death."

which he said was from the Mayor, then proceeded to read aloud portions of it in violent language. Sister Constance listened to each man's complaint, and then said with great calmness and gentleness, 'Sirs, is it possible that you would have us refuse to these children the very protection you have obtained for your own? We do not propose to make a hospital of the Asylum; if any of the children are taken ill with the fever, they shall be carried immediately to our Infirmary at the Church Home.' Her words, and still more I think her gentle, sweet tones, produced a marked effect upon the excited men. Noticing this, I said quickly, 'Are you not willing to trust the sisters?' A few said, 'Yes, we are,' and all gave way, when my Sister ordered the driver to proceed. The next day we opened the house, and, in twenty-four hours, received twenty-six orphans; in four days there were fifty children in the asylum. (*Sisters of St. Mary's at Memphis*, author unknown)

Sister Constance wrote daily letters to Mother Harriet in New York, which revealed their problems and perplexities.

They sent us orphans so fast that we cannot keep them in the one outside room we dare to use here ... We have taken the Canfield Asylum and are fitting it up roughly for them as a sort of quarantine house, carrying them over to the Home as fast as we dare ... Yesterday, I found two young girls, who had spent two days in a two-room cottage with the unburied bodies of their parents, their uncle in the utmost suffering and delirium, and no one near them but a rough negro drayman who held the sick man in his bed. It was twenty-four hours before I could get those two fearful corpses buried, and then I had to send for a police officer to the board of Health, before any undertaker would enter that room. One grows perfectly hardened to these things—carts with eight or nine corpses in rough boxes, are ordinary sights. I saw a nurse stop one to-day and ask for a certain man's residence—the negro driver just pointed over his shoulder with his whip at the heap of coffins behind him and answered, 'I've got him here in his coffin.'

According to Sister Mary Hilary, by the end of the summer, the death rate reached 70 in one day. Understandably, the Sisters' concern was much more for the victims than for the cause of the disease. Few nurses were available, and the Sisters worked constantly taking care of the ill. They answered call after call. One call came to Sister Constance, which was particularly heart-rending. A man gave her a telegram and insisted she read it. It was a plea for help from a young girl:

"Father and mother are lying dead in the house, brother is dying send me some help, no money." Sister Constance immediately responded to the call and found a young girl in mourning. "There was a corpse on the sofa, another one on a bed, and a delirious nearly naked young man rocking himself back and forth in agony."

Many eagerly volunteered, but it was finally decided to send Sister Ruth and Sister Helen to Memphis because both had experience nursing at the Trinity Parish Infirmary. When Sister Ruth heard that she had been selected, her reply came quickly, "Pray for me, that in life, in death, I may be ever his own." Arriving on September 2, 1878, they went immediately to the Asylum to work.

The next sad development was the illness of the Reverend Charles C. Parsons, Canon of the Cathedral. The illnesses of both Dean Harris and Mr. Parsons made it impossible for the Sisters to handle all the calls for help that were thrust upon them. Part of a letter from Sister Constance to Mother Harriet again describes the horrors that surrounded them:

> The calls for food and wine are incessant. I have been on my feet almost the whole day, for our old cook would not do a thing if one of us did not stay with her, whenever we could be spared from the sick. A nurse has just been here to say that he will not stay another night with his two patients—a father and daughter—if the dead mother is not buried. The body has been there for nearly two days, and no undertaker can be found who has time to bring a coffin. We are absolutely forbidden to touch the dead even if a coffin could be found. Dr. Harris is all that earthly strength can be to us, but he is far from strong. I do not think he even hopes to get through. Pray doubly for us now, dear mother.

Davis recorded this heart-rending statement, mailed by George C. Harris, Dean, and Charles C. Parsons to the Rector of St. Lazarus and Grace Church in New York, which expresses the depth of their needs:

> To feed the hungry, To provide the barest necessities of the sick, To minister to the dying, To bury the dead, To take immediate care of the orphans made so by the ravages of the fever ... To meet these requirements we have absolutely nothing, and there is nothing that we can look for, unless

George C. Harris, Dean of St. Mary's Cathedral, 1873-1880. Overwhelmed by all their work, the Sisters wrote to the Mother House asking for help. The illness of George C. Harris, Dean of the Cathedral, increased the responsibilities for the women. According to Sister Constance, "He was the wise and holy priest upon whom we depended daily for direction, and for much of our strength."

the hearts of our brethren are touched by this plain statement of our wants … In this view we offer an appeal for aid from all who are able to give us help.

From almost every corner of the United States, and even from England, Canada, Germany, and France, came responses to their cry for assistance. Priests, physicians, and churches volunteered to give aid both financially and in person. Many became martyrs to the cause of assisting the victims of this dreadful disease.

Because of the illnesses of both Dean Harris and Mr. Parsons, there were no priests available to help the Sisters and no daily celebration of the Holy Eucharist. Sister Mary Hilary notes that their need of the priests' physical and spiritual strength made it extremely difficult for the Sisters to answer all the calls that came to them. On September 3, Bishop Quintard visited his very good friend, Dean Harris, who recovered from the disease, but sadly, Mr. Parsons died on September 7th, a victim of this dread pestilence. Sister Ruth was devastated by the news of Mr. Parsons' death, and she wrote to Mother Harriet describing his death and burial. "His body had to be placed in the family vault of Mrs. Bullock, a devoted associate, for it was impossible to fill all the demands for graves." In this same letter, she asked for the following: rubber sheets, a scrubbing brush, a dustpan, and prayers. She concluded with the following: "I have just whipped a big boy for tying up a goose & beating it, & filling the babies mouths with red pepper. With forty such children our hands are full." This all occurred on the very same day Sister Constance and Sister Thecla came down with the fever. Sister Constance took care of Dean Harris, even though she herself was ill; however, she finally reached the end of her strength. Dean Harris later attributed his recovery to Sister Constance's vigil by his bedside. One of the Sisters discovered her lying on a couch and realized immediately the seriousness of her illness.

> I knew at once that she was very ill. She insisted that it was only a slight headache, and would not listen to my entreaties that she would go to bed, but continued dictating letters … Her face was flushed with fever ... She talked of resuming her work among the sick as soon as possible … They were about to place her on a comfortable mattress; she refused saying, 'It is the only one you have in the house, and if I have the fever you will have to burn it.' The same day Thecla came down with the fever and like

This is from notes of Bishop Quintard concerning the yellow fever epidemic of 1878. University of the South Archives, Sewanee, Tennessee.

Constance refused to lie down on the mattress. The same practical spirit animated these two brave, thoughtful women.

Sister Ruth's letter to Mother Harriet relates hearing Sister Constance's low moan all through the evening:

> About midnight, she said, 'Hosanna,' repeating it again and again more faintly. This was the last word. But still she continued the low soft moan of one unconscious, though not in pain, till at 7 A.M., St. Mary's bell rang out on the air. At that clear sound which she had always loved, whose call she had never refused to answer, the moaning ceased; and at 10 o'clock her soul entered the Paradise of Perfect Love.

The fever spread rapidly among the Sisters. Sister Thecla died on September 12th and Sister Ruth on the 18th—living only a few days after she arrived in Memphis. Although Sister Hughetta became ill, she survived, but shortly thereafter Sister Francis, stricken for the second time by the fever, died October 4th. The death of these Sisters elicited a great deal of publicity, causing newspapers all over the country to carry the news of their deaths, emphasizing and praising their service to the community of Memphis.

Those assisting in the consecration were Bishop Quintard, assisted by Dean Harris, the Reverend George Moore of Somerville, and Thomas F. Gailor, a young deacon at Pulaski, who later became Bishop of Tennessee. The text for Dean Harris' sermon was "He feedeth among the lilies." He concluded his remarks by "explaining that the last words of Sister Constance were 'Alleluia Osanna, the triumphant shout of the redeemed.'"

At the 1879 convention, Bishop Quintard expressed his thankfulness for all who had served—clergy, Sisters, and laymen—in the yellow fever epidemic. A full-page tribute was carried in the *Diocesan Journal*.

After the yellow fever epidemic of 1878, Mother Harriet was deeply concerned about the Sisters remaining in Memphis, for the city was in dark despair, and she questioned whether a school could be successful during that particular time. Sister Hughetta had other ideas and entreated Mother Harriet to continue her support of St. Mary's. One reason was probably Sister Hughetta's connection to the Snowden family in Memphis, and the other was her desire for "St. Mary's School to continue its tradition of quality education, of which she wanted to remain a part." Reluctantly, Mother Harriet agreed.

Following their deaths, Bishop Quintard began raising money to build an altar at the Cathedral in their memory. This altar was first installed in the wooden cathedral in May and was consecrated on Whitsunday, June 1, 1879. Dr. John Henry Hopkins describes the altar as follows:

> *The altar rests upon a platform of dove colored marble, of three steps, with risers of Tennessee marble. On the lowest riser is the legend:* † *Sisters of St. Mary* † *September and October 1878* †. *On the riser of the second step are the four names:* † *Constance* † *Thecla* † *Ruth* † *Frances. On the upper riser these words from the Song of Solomon:* † *'He feedeth among lilies … '*. *The bottom shelf of the retable is carved with foliage and the risers are of Tennessee marble with the legend on the gospel side* Alleluia Osanna *and on the epistle side* Osanna Alleluia.

Sister Hughetta was a remarkable woman. She was born in 1848 in Nashville, the seventh child of John Bayard Snowden and Aspasia Seraphina (Imogene) Bogardus Snowden, whose first American ancestors came to this country in the 1600s. After the death of her father, her mother, Aspasia, moved the family to New York City. Aspasia was a very vital person—a real grande dame of New York society. She was horrified to hear that her talented and beautiful youngest daughter had a "call" to retire from worldly affairs to become a nun. She ordered Hughetta never to mention the matter again until one year after a formal debut had been made to give her a taste of living a "normal" life. But the "call" was a real one, and at the year's end, she entered the community of Sisters. She completed her novitiate in Memphis and became a full Sister in 1878; then came her baptism by fire. Sister Hughetta was the only one of the original four Sisters who survived the yellow fever epidemic and was later appointed Sister Superior of the Southern Community. She seemed to have a natural gift for administration because she not only saw to it that St. Mary's became a vital force for education in Memphis, but also in 1888, she established S. Mary's-on-the-Mountain at Sewanee as a rest home for the Sisters, and later as the school and seat of missionary work for the mountaineers.

St. Mary's prospered under Sister Hughetta's leadership despite competition from two local private schools for girls, Miss Higbee's and the Clara Conway School. In a report to the Episcopal Convention in 1888, St. Mary's enrollment consisted of ninety girls; twenty-six were boarding pupils.

St. Mary's, however, never equaled the enrollment of the Conway Institute or the Higbee School (the latter surviving until 1914 and the Clara Conway School until the turn of the century), but St. Mary's outlasted them and continued to offer a fine college preparatory education. Sisters Hughetta, Flora, and Herberta were members of the faculty, as were lay teachers, Florence Dewsnap, Marion Boyle, Susan Baylor Temple, Maud A. Stowe, Mary L. Beecher, Carrie Keating, Professor Paul Schneider, Professor Louis Bignou, and Miss A. Stephenson.

The 1880s and 1890s proved to be an excellent time for St. Mary's to grow and develop. As calamities in other great cities in America had resulted in a rebirth, so the end of the yellow fever epidemic in Memphis led to a city that was ready for development. The

St. Mary's students, May 1881.

National Board of Health surveyed existing conditions and gave recommendations to the local officials resulting in a new sewage system, ninety-five miles of hard pavement, the discovery of artesian water, the inauguration of a waste disposal service, an isolation hospital, telephone lines, electric lights, and an electrified antiquated street railway system. Many new public buildings, churches, and hotels were built. The Tennessee Club and the Grand Opera both appeared in the '80s. There was a large increase in population, cotton became king, and the economy grew. Additionally, "The value of land increased from 48 million to 250 million dollars," according to Gerald M. Capers, Jr.

A burgeoning demand for the education of women resulted in considerable competition between girls' schools. Sister Hughetta's rather surprising report, entitled "Athletic Lassies," revealed a growing interest in gymnastics. She presented "The Olympic Exercises of the Pupils of St. Mary's School" to the Diocesan Board:

> Yesterday afternoon the pupils of St. Mary's School gave a gymnastic exhibition. A large number of the patrons of the school were present, all of whom were greatly pleased with the program of the young ladies. The exercises were

designed to develop the strength and muscles, and Miss Emerson is to be greatly commended for the degree of perfection attained by her pupils in marching and in using the dumb bells. In the language of Dr. Burford (Rector of Calvary Church) who was present and spoke a few words of praise: 'St. Mary's School never undertakes anything without making a success of it.'

Sister Hughetta made another interesting report to the Diocesan Convention in 1888, "A certain amount of gymnastic exercise was a part of the daily routine ... [and] its wholesome effects were visible." Later, she remarked, "The school desired to keep fully abreast of the times and to make use of all that is good in the so-called new education." (Their rival, Clara Conway specialized in the "new education"!)

The faculty, circa 1890s. Sister Hughetta is in the center.

Obviously there was competition between these schools and perhaps some disagreement about their educational philosophy. It does seem possible that Sister Hughetta was influenced a little by this "new education" for she added, "For the ensuing year, increased advantages will be secured, such as a more complete apparatus, a chemical laboratory, a valuable herbarium, and additions to the library." The success of the school was no doubt due to a willingness to search for new ideas and ways to improve the curriculum, always undergirded by a dedication to academic excellence and to the spiritual life. Enrollment was around one hundred, including twenty to thirty boarding students; the cost of St. Mary's was board $200 and tuition $40 upward, depending on the course of study.

Two new buildings were constructed, one a three story brick school completed on Poplar in 1888, and a Chapel, both just east of the Cathedral. This beautiful little building, completed in 1887, and called the Sisters' Chapel, was donated by Colonel Robert Snowden, Sister Hughetta's brother, and was dedicated in memory of their mother, Mrs. John Bayard Snowden. Bishop Quintard consecrated the chapel in 1888.

St. Mary's Episcopal School, east of the Cathedral, 366 Poplar Street.

Many graduates of the school have held their wedding ceremonies in this chapel, perhaps cherishing and remembering their moments in chapel throughout their school years at St. Mary's.

When it was necessary to tear down the school building, the chapel was preserved due to the foresight of Bayard Cairns, the Cathedral architect. It had the same stone as the Cathedral, and on May 19, 1932, was dedicated to the memory of Aspasia Seraphina (Imogene) Bogardus Snowden and Mary Joy Snowden Cairns, the grandmother and mother of Mr. Cairns.

Today, this beautiful chapel is visited each year by elementary school students of St. Mary's, reminding them of the Sisters' dedication to service in the community and to St. Mary's School.

St. Mary's students, 1890s.

Notices in *The Commercial Appeal* about St. Mary's in the 1890s differ in subject matter and tone from the ones in today's newspapers. Their purpose was the same as that of the advertisements of today—to let the public know the activities of the school. These ads all appeared in *The Commercial Appeal's* column, "100 Years Ago:"

May 28, 1891 — The Young Ladies of St. Mary's, 366 Poplar, will give a beautiful entertainment this evening at 5 o'clock. Music, poetry, and art will be blended in one harmonious whole. The tableaux are almost entirely Grecian, and will be carried out in all their artistic effects.

June 5, 1891 — The Sisters of St. Mary's held their commencement yesterday morning. The study-room was decorated with half blown magnolia buds, a fit type of the fair young bud being sent out on the journey of life. The graduates were Elizabeth Mosby, Margaret Gray, Matilda Reid, Lizzie F. Faxon. The exercises were followed by a reception in the parlors.

Sept. 12, 1892 — St. Mary's School — 366 Poplar — Fall term begins September 21st. Miss S.B. Temple will be in charge of the Department of Higher English; Miss N.M. Gaige of Elocution and Physical Culture; Miss Helen Leigh Steward, of Natural Science and Latin; Miss Electa Boyle, of Arithmetic; Miss Freeman, of Penmanship; Prof. Roder, of French; Sister Caroline, of Higher Mathematics and History, Sister Herberta, of the Kindergarten School; Miss Louise Finley, the Primary Department.

August 1, 1893 — Tomorrow at Sewanee, Tenn. The Reverend Thomas Frank Gailor, vice-chancellor of the University of the South, will be consecrated as bishop coadjutor of Tennessee, to serve in aid of the Rt. Reverend Bishop C.T. Quintard of the Episcopal Church. The Reverend Mr. Gailor is the only son of the late Frank Gailor, editor of the pre-war *Memphis Daily Avalanche*, who lost his life in the battle of Perryville, Ky., in 1862.

One of St. Mary's most treasured traditions, May Day, began when the Sisters were in charge of the school. Although it has changed throughout the years, queens, princesses, ladies-in- waiting, and pages have played a major role in the festivities. The May Queen is a junior, elected by members of the Upper School, and the princess is a sixth grader elected by her class. A ring is passed down

Ann Blanche Steele, early May Queen.

each year, from the previous May Queen to the newly elected Queen, which she wears during her year as Queen. Dancing was a major part of the program, for many years either "on the green," around a maypole, or in later years, in the gymnasium.

In 1990, the name was changed to Spring Fest, and is presided over by a Queen, a Princess, and the court, consisting of members of the junior class. The festivities are now held in the Church of the Holy Communion, with students entertaining the Queen and her court.

In 1893, an important election was held that profoundly affected the school. The Reverend Thomas Frank Gailor, a native of Memphis, became Bishop Coadjutor, to serve under Bishop Quintard.

He was elected on the first ballot and became the third Bishop of the Diocese of Tennessee, February 15, 1898, and was a great

Thomas Gailor, S.T.D., LL.D., Bishop of Tennessee, 1898-1935, pictured right, authored St. Mary's School Prayer:

> Almighty God, Fountain of all wisdom, be with us, we pray thee, in our work today. Endue all the teachers with a sense of their responsibility, and with grace and strength for its fulfillment. Keep the students in health of mind and soul and body; make them diligent in study, guard their inexperience, and save them through all temptations. Bless the patrons and alumnae of this school, and enable us all, more and more each day, to advance in that knowledge which is eternal life. Through Jesus Christ our Lord. Amen.

supporter and advocate of the school. He wrote the following statement about the school, which has been quoted many times: "They believe that in the long run it pays to be honest, to be thorough, and not to pander to the popular demand for the mere social veneering, which some people call 'the education of girls.'" He is also particularly remembered for the gift of his beautiful prayer written for St. Mary's School, which is prayed every morning in chapel and at all special occasions.

1895 marks the birth of *St. Mary's Scroll*, and while it is not the first school newspaper (*The Bouquet* was published in 1866), it indeed has left an indelible mark. On the cover of this 1895 issue is a picture of Bishop F. Gailor, Assistant Bishop of Tennessee, and on the back cover is a picture of the school advertising St. Mary's School as a

A page from St. Mary's Scroll.

ST. MARY'S SCHOOL,

A Boarding and Day-School for Girls.

——UNDER THE CHARGE OF THE——

SISTERS OF ST. MARY OF THE EPISCOPAL CHURCH,
364-366 Poplar St. Memphis, Tenn.

The students receive a large share of individual instruction. They are under the constant care of the Sisters, who give their lives to the work, for Christ's sake. Their aim is to train those who are entrusted to their care, morally, intellectually and physically—to develope together the faculties of the heart and soul, mind and body, not depreciating any part of the nature God has made.

They do not measure their success by the extent, but by the thoroughness of their work. They rather look forward to the gradual development of a heightened education, than rest in what has been accomplished.

St. Mary's has a most able corps of instructors.

Prof. A. M. Merrill (Graduate of Dickerson College, Pa.), Literature Rhetoric History and Geometry.
Prof. Wm. Messick (Graduate of Yale,) Greek and Latin.
Mrs. Annie Sale, Algebra and English Grammar.
Mrs. Malcolm McDowell (Wellesley), Natural Science.
Miss Electa Boyle (Graduate of St. Mary's School, Memphis,) Arithmetic and English.
Miss Effie Tucker (Graduate of New York School of Elocution), Physical Culture and Elocution.
M. Paul Rodet (Paris, France), French.
Miss Carrie Richardson (Graduate of Boston Conservatory of Music), Piano.
Mrs. Cary Anderson Voice.
Prof. Snider, Violin.
Miss Solari (Florence, Italy), Drawing and Painting.

The Sisters teach throughout the School. Frequent lectures are given during the School year by eminent lecturers. With its advanced methods of education St. Mary's School prepares students for any college to which women are admitted. Many of its graduates are now employed as successful teachers.

For a Catalogue of the School, Apply to the

SISTER SUPERIOR.

Graduation announcement, 1897.

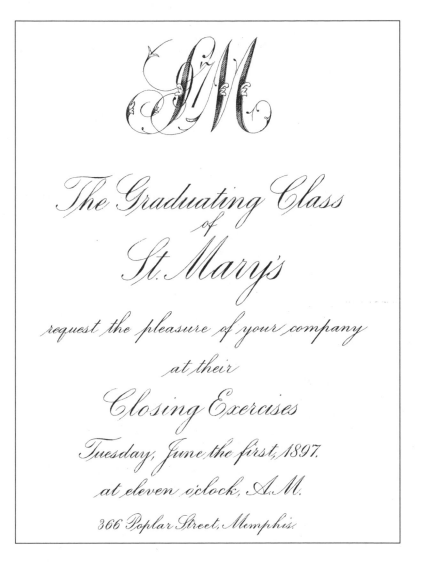

SM

The Graduating Class
of
St. Mary's

request the pleasure of your company

at their

Closing Exercises

Tuesday, June the first, 1897.

at eleven o'clock, A.M.

366 Poplar Street, Memphis.

Boarding and Day-School for Girls, under the charge of the Sisters of St. Mary of the Episcopal Church, 364-366 Poplar Street. The purpose of *St. Mary's Scroll* was to uncover some of the literary talent in our "Rosebud Garden of Girls."

The list of editors of the newspaper contains some familiar Memphis names: Lila Payne Carnes and Annie Snowden, Editors-in-Chief; Jeanie Rees Lea, Local Editor; Grace Gwendolynn Everman, Literary Editor; Sue Rose Crook, Exchange Editor; Belle James Willis, Alumnae Editor. Business Managers were Corinne Goodman Boyle, Sarah Wallace Sledge, Maria Louise Fleece, and Elizabeth Elvira Dix.

The editor explained how the name "St. Mary's Scroll" came to be:

> *It would not be like the rolls and scrolls of olden times which were illuminated by skillful hands in gold and cobalt blues and emerald green … but we hope to give you the record of some golden deeds, the crimson flushes of the thoughts of our hearts; bits of azure blue, and yes, it is inevitable, the little green things too. Over these last we will strive to run a tracery of the fine silver fret-work of charity, as the old painters did, brightening and beautifying the dull and the faulty with fine drawn lines of silver and gold.*

Naming the new literary magazine required many hours of discussion. Some of the suggestions considered were the merits of "owlets," "chimes," and "flower wreaths." Finally, the staff decided to accept the choice of Bishop Gailor and called it *St. Mary's Scroll*.

The only other publication during the Sisters' administration available in the archives is entitled *The Twentieth Century Tatler*, dated May 1903. The editor-in-chief was Helen D. Freeman, and her staff included many well known Memphis names: Virginia Heiskell, Katharine Edgington, Pauline Bridge, Mary Love, Beatrix M. Fortune, Olivette Sledge, and Gertrude Fortune.

It mostly contained essays about famous authors, yet also included a few personal ones, such as "The Mississippi at Sunset." The size of *The Tatler* was much smaller, more similar to *Belles Lettres*, the literary magazine of today, than to the present *The Tatler*, which is filled with current happenings. *The Tatler* of 1903 did include some tongue in cheek current events, revealing that the students were not lacking in a sense of humor:

> Mad Mullah, who is giving the British so much trouble, is no kin to the Maud Muller, who raked the hay.

> The asphalt pavement on Poplar Street, now nearly completed, is a thing of beauty, and we hope it may prove to be a joy forever.

> The City Directory men have reported that Memphis has a population of about 160,000 inhabitants. The growth of Memphis is phenomenal. It now has the vim and push of Chicago, the culture of Boston, the beauty and wit of Louisville, and a large amount of the weinerwurst and sauerkraut of St. Louis.

Furthermore, St. Mary's evidently had an exchange program of periodicals with other schools, for critiques of these are included:

> *The Georgia Tech*, an attractive semi-weekly periodical, comes to us regularly. The locals, to use a slang expression, are 'awfully cute.'

> *The University of Arizona Magazine*, or, in other words, the *Cyanide Process*, must be very interesting to those who have studied this subject, but to girls still in preparatory schools the process seems abstruse.

The Tatler also contained advertisements from Goldsmith's, Brodnax Jewelers, Fortune-Ward Drug Company, D. Canale & Co.

Memphis Steam Laundry, and others, all familiar names to Memphis.

A boarding department was alive and active during the years the Sisters were in charge of St. Mary's. Usually, there were approximately twenty-five boarders, and the rules for these boarding students were strict and enforced. According to one source:

> They were instructed to keep their apartments in order, to mend their clothes, and were taught that high intellectual culture cannot preclude the necessity of being skilled and graceful in the discharge of the plain duties of home and social life.

Once a month they were allowed to spend Saturday and Sunday with their parents. Some interesting and humorous memories about life at St. Mary's are recorded by Mary Kirk Adams '07, in her article, "Remembrances of a Boarding Pupil at St. Mary's, 1904-07":

> At fourteen years of age, Papa took me to Memphis and turned me over to the Sisters of St. Mary's School on Poplar … My sketchy schooling had been at grandma Warfield's knee, sitting on a stool. She was more interested in my French and music Lesson and I in the great outdoors. The carefree little girl from a Delta Plantation was transplanted in the brick walls of the building next to the crypt—that was the beginning of St. Mary's Cathedral—with the dignified, religious, wonderful Sisters of St. Mary's. I loved it all … My roommate, Mildred Sledge from Como, was also at a disadvantage, having had no public schooling, and we struggled, even cried over 'paper hanging' in arithmetic. It wasn't until Miss Willie Johnson took us over in algebra that she opened up the wonders of mathematics.

> Sister Mary Maud was the Sister in charge. Sister Roberta, so beautiful and sad, we decided that she had been disappointed in love, then a long, tall hippy sister named Herberta … One time in the dormitory as Sister Herberta came through the door I doused her with a pitcher of water … I thought she was someone else. I grabbed her and kissed her but she gave me two weeks silence.

> Our schedule for the day was: first, the rising bell; then the assembly bell; two by two we marched into the chapel for morning prayer; breakfast, a blessing before and after; clean our rooms, classes, then lunch and more classes and study period; play time until 5:00 p.m., evening service; our favorite song was 'Now the Day is Over;' another study hour and then to bed with all the lights off.

The association with the Sisters of St. Mary's, the academic and religious training will always be a blessed heritage.

One by one the Sisters withdrew from St. Mary's, some to St. Gabriel's School, Peekskill, and one to become head of the Order of Sisters of St. Mary in the Southwest. Under the direction and authority of Bishop Gailor, the school was entrusted to the direction of two lay teachers, Miss Helen Loomis and Miss Mary Paoli. The following are remarks made by Bishop Gailor at that time:

> I agreed to take the school under my official supervision provided it was put on the same basis as our diocesan schools with the Bishop as ex-officio chairman of the Board of Visitors, and a clergyman of the church made chaplain and responsible for religious instruction.

Edith and Emily James, students 1885-1906.

Mary Raines '04, great grand-mother of Lauren Maddux '98 and Jenny Maddux '01.

By the end of 1911, Bishop Gailor was able to announce to the Diocesan Convention that the property had been purchased from the Sisterhood:

> *By the generosity of the people of Memphis I have been able to buy the property of St. Mary's School ... The Sisterhood of St. Mary's after thirty-eight years ... withdrew ... during the past year.*

At the Commencement service that year, he spoke "gratefully of the work done by the Sisterhood ... [and] expressed regret at their withdrawal and offered words of encouragement to the new management."

The land with the brick School building, the Sisters' House, and the Chapel buildings were transferred to the control of the Diocese with the title vested in Bishop Gailor.

Few schools anywhere have a more dramatic story to tell. The Sisters' emphasis on academic excellence and their dedication to service continues to be a challenge to those who study and teach at St.

*Sisters from Sewanee visit
St. Mary's.*

Mary's. Each year, there is a service dedicated to the Martyrs of
Memphis at St. Mary's Cathedral. In 1996, the class of 2003 was so
touched by the story of the Sisters' lives, and especially by the
purchase of the chalice in 1873, that they made beautiful felt chalices
for the chasubles of the Right Reverend Bishop James Coleman and
for the St. Mary's School's Chaplain, the Reverend Mary Katherine
Allman, as well as planned a service honoring the Martyrs of
Memphis. On September 9, 1996, these students led the service, and
Bishop Coleman gave a homily about the lives of the Sisters. A
Eucharist followed, the participants drinking from the same chalice
bought by the Sisters one hundred and twenty-three years ago. Since
1910, the chalice has resided first at St. Mary's School on the
Mountain and then with the Sisters, who have a Retreat Center in
Sewanee. This service was memorable, tying the past to the present
and reminding both students and faculty of the spiritual thread that
binds St. Mary's School together.

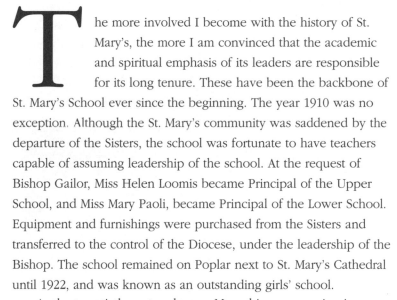

3. ENDURANCE THROUGH TUMULTUOUS YEARS

T he more involved I become with the history of St. Mary's, the more I am convinced that the academic and spiritual emphasis of its leaders are responsible for its long tenure. These have been the backbone of St. Mary's School ever since the beginning. The year 1910 was no exception. Although the St. Mary's community was saddened by the departure of the Sisters, the school was fortunate to have teachers capable of assuming leadership of the school. At the request of Bishop Gailor, Miss Helen Loomis became Principal of the Upper School, and Miss Mary Paoli, became Principal of the Lower School. Equipment and furnishings were purchased from the Sisters and transferred to the control of the Diocese, under the leadership of the Bishop. The school remained on Poplar next to St. Mary's Cathedral until 1922, and was known as an outstanding girls' school.

As the twentieth century began, Memphis was growing in population as well as in area. The Board of Park Commissioners was initiated in 1900; one of their first acts was to oversee the purchase of a large tract of land, named Overton Park. There was a real change in transportation: automobiles arrived in Memphis, streets were planned, airplanes began to appear, efforts were made to clean up the city, community services were increased, and motorized fire engines replaced the horse-drawn ones. Hardwood became the second most important industry in Memphis. Similar to cotton, it was

Miss Helen Loomis, about 1910.

Miss Helen Loomis, Upper School Principal, 1910-1949.

Miss Paoli and Miss Loomis, drawn by Dorothy Summerfield when she was in 10th grade at St. Mary's.

responsible for the development of many new industries—the manufacturing of barrels, boxes, doors, and wagons, to mention a few. In the late 1800s, Memphis was introduced to its first street railway car system running on Main, Jefferson, and Poplar. According to Robert A. Sigafoos:

> The spatial pattern changed dramatically when the electrically powered streetcars made their appearance ... Memphis was opened up for land development on the periphery ... and real estate developers seized the opportunity and started the suburban movement which ran practically unabated until the Great Depression in the 1930s.

All this had its effect on St. Mary's. As the city was growing and prospering, these years provided a propitious time for a private school to be in demand as well as to grow and be successful.

Unfortunately, St. Mary's has few official records existing for the years 1910-1949, the latter being the year Miss Loomis and Miss Neely retired from the school. However, there are artifacts collected from alumnae: brochures, report cards, commencement invitations and pictures. Nevertheless, no transcripts or records of students attending during these years remain. Although memories of Miss Loomis do abound in the minds and hearts of alumnae and friends

and in a few newspaper accounts, sadly, very limited facts about Miss Paoli or her contributions to St. Mary's are in existence. A brochure published in 1921 mentions that "Miss Paoli, who has charge of the Primary department, holds the certificate granted to those who successfully complete a training course in the Montessori method under accredited teachers." A few reports were made by Bishop Gailor to the Diocese during these years, which disclosed information about the school. The first one, given in 1914, contained a complimentary statement about Miss Paoli and Miss Loomis:

> Under the efficient direction of Miss Helen Loomis and Miss Mary Harris Paoli, and the spiritualities of which are under the oversight of Dean Morris, of the Cathedral, [Bishop Gailor] has sent in an encouraging report ... The statistics for the current year are as follows: Ninety students enrolled; teachers, exclusive of specials in music, nine. Finances: school entirely self-supporting and independent. Property: rented from the Church from the Bishop. We stand as a church school although one-half of our patronage is from without the Church.

The second report appeared in the 1915 Diocesan Report and gave some additional information about these years:

> St. Mary's School ... continues to lead among the private schools of the city, although it no longer receives resident pupils in the building. The title of the property is now vested in Bishop Gailor. There is no endowment, but the high character of the work done should insure the continued prosperity of the school ... Twenty-eight girls from the College Preparatory Department have entered colleges in the South and Vassar, Smith, Wellesley, and Cornell in the East. Some of these have been elected to Phi Beta Kappa and have attained other honors.

Interesting insights about the school in the early part of the twentieth century have been revealed by correspondence from alumnae who graduated during those years. Lucia Burch Vinton '10, a graduate of Vassar College, expressed her enjoyment of her years at the school, adding that "my preparation at St. Mary's was so excellent that my freshman year of college was actually easy for me." A note from Fannie Eldredge King '13 "recollects the line of veiled girls marching into chapel by music played by Miss Mattie Reid and Miss Oliver." Another graduate of the class of 1913, Ida Myrtle Hays

A delightful visit with Margaret Boyle Falls '15 revealed some of her thoughts about her years at St. Mary's. She has fond memories of Bishop Gailor and the influence of his chapel talks on her life. She talked about her classmates, seven of whom became lifelong friends. They belonged to a club entitled GFC. The club had no officers, no duties, no new members, but lots of fun. They never told anyone outside the club the meaning of GFC. When I asked her if she would tell me, she said emphatically, "I'll never tell."

Triumphant basketball team of 1913.

St. Mary's Cheer between 1910-1914:

   1 a zizzy
   2 a zizzy
   3 a zizzy zam
   St. Mary's girls don't
   give a (pause)
   razzel dazzel,
   hobble gobble,
   siz boom bah —
   St. Mary's, St. Mary's
   rah! rah! rah!

White, wrote that her "graduating class consisted of six students," and continued her note by writing "how proud I am of St. Mary's."

Interestingly, athletics was also a part of the life of the school during these years. Their main rival in basketball was Miss Higbee's School as evidenced by photographs and a newspaper headline that reads: "Triumphant St. Mary's Squad and Higbee Team Which Disputed Victory."

Also, residing in St. Mary's archives is a picture of the 1913 basketball team (above). One member of this team later commented, "We were not too successful, but what we lacked in skill, we made up for in enthusiasm."

The year 1922 produced two changes which had tremendous impact on the school. The first was the necessity for a new Lower School Principal. Miss Mary Paoli died in 1922; her death dropped a veil of sadness on the entire school. A sentence in Bishop Gailor's

Mary Paoli's name is kept alive at St. Mary's by an award given each year in her memory to an eighth grade student with the highest scholastic average over two years.

Miss Katherine Neely, Principal of Lower School, 1922-1949.

diary at the time of Miss Paoli's death emphasized his personal feelings about her and her importance to the school:

> Miss Paoli was a woman of the finest intelligence, and a loyal daughter of the church. Her loss to the school is almost irreparable. A host of friends lament her death. Mrs. Gilmore Lynn, former teacher under Miss Paoli and late Principal and now Principal Emeritus, mentions Miss Paoli in her memoirs about the school and recalls 'she was dearly loved and her death was a great loss to the school.'

It was a difficult time for the school, but fortunately Miss Katherine Neely, a teacher in the elementary school, was eminently qualified to be Principal of the Lower School.

The second change was one of location. A document of incorporation important to St. Mary's was written in 1922 and presented to the Diocesan Convention, clarifying the relationship between the church and the school, which, according to Bishop Gailor, was "to preserve the Church's control over the school without committing the Convention any obligation for financial support."

At that time, it became obvious that the school needed more room and better facilities. Many patrons agreed and encouraged a move to a better location. It was the school's good fortune to find property appropriate and available for a school at 1257 Poplar, across from the present location of Tech High. The following detailed report

St. Mary's at 1257 Poplar, 1922.

about the planned move was given to the Education Committee of the Diocese:

> For many years of honorable service it was found three years ago impossible to carry on satisfactorily the work of St. Mary's School in the old location at 714 Poplar Avenue, next door to the Cathedral; and a movement was started to secure another site for the school with more extensive grounds. It was a testimony to the good standing of the school that many patrons and friends, some of them not members of the Episcopal Church, made contributions sufficiently large for us to purchase a very spacious and beautiful school property farther out on the Poplar Boulevard, as there was not enough money in hand to pay for the property and a debt had to be incurred, it was decided to incorporate the school and thus carry the debt. By the wise and careful guidance and help of Judge Charles N. Burch, this was accomplished and the property was secured.
>
> The charter provides that the Bishop of Tennessee shall be the President of the corporation, and the other members shall be appointed by the Bishop, subject to the approval of the Diocesan Convention. The trustees are therefore only a holding corporation for the Episcopal Church in the Diocese of Tennessee.
>
> A contract for ten years was made with Miss Helen A. Loomis to carry on the school at a fixed salary—the contract to be terminated by either party at six months' notice.
>
> I am glad to report that the school is in excellent condition, financially and otherwise. The Dean of the Cathedral is Chaplain of the school; daily services are held, and religious instruction is regularly given.

The property at 1257 Poplar was purchased on June 8, 1923. This new and larger home was cause for excitement for everyone connected with the school. Lovely grounds surrounded the building, providing an ideal setting. A wing was added to the east side of the residence, making room on the first floor for a dining room and on the second floor for a dormitory. About 100 feet south of the residence, a one-and-a-half story building was erected, containing a center hall with classrooms on either side. It was extremely up-to-date for each classroom even had its own outside door in case of fire or the hated monthly fire drill. The attic of this building was spacious

Mary Brewster Napolski '35, in a letter in 1991 to the alumnae, described some of her recollections:

I have happy memories of daily chapel in the school attic, where Principal Helen Loomis led the reverent meeting. Under the eaves of the attic were the big cardboard boxes of interesting costumes for the Shakespeare plays we performed on the attic stage, to enthusiastic audiences. On inclement days we had our vigorous aesthetic dancing classes in the attic instead of the grassy yard.

A program for A Midsummer Night's Dream.

and was put to use instantly and constantly by the students for their extracurricular activities. In our archives, I discovered an interesting program for a play entitled *The Red Tsar*, produced by Charlotte Gailor and Alumnae of St. Mary's Episcopal School, which was presented at the Lyric Theater on November 23, 1922.

Apparently drama was one of the favorite activities of the school during these years. Plays such as *Deirdre*, A *Midsummer Night's Dream*, and *King Alfred's Jewel* were performed in the attic. The acting group's official name was "The Attic Players of St. Mary's School."

Gwen Robinson Awsumb '32 was chosen as St. Mary's outstanding alumna in 1996. In a talk to the students, she inspired and encouraged her audience:

The St. Mary's I attended was very different from the one you are attending. The building was one-story with an attic where we had chapel every morning before class. There was no altar, no beautiful blue reredos, no light streaming through the windows. It was dark and dingy, but the prayers we said got us started for the day ... There were no computers [and] no calculators … but strange as it may seem, we managed to muddle through because we did have one thing going for us—and it still goes for you—the basic standard of excellence … We were challenged, just as you are, and we were expected to do our very best, just as you

arc. The goal was clear. The goal was always excellence and it still is ... One thing is very different ... the choices for my future were vastly limited ... You can actually be almost anything you set your mind to because the women who preceded you opened those (closed) doors ... When I ran for office 40 years ago, there had never been a woman elected to the ruling body of the city ... One day during your lifetime, there could well be a woman President of this country ... Why not a St. Mary's alum as President of the United States? Whatever road opens to you ... the background you have received here at St. Mary's will have prepared you for traveling down that road with confidence in yourself and faith in your God. Nothing else matters.

Another alumna, Anne Howard Bailey '41, has written for many well-known television series, such as *General Hospital*, *Family*, *Bonanza*, and *Lassie*, and an opera libretto, *Deseret*. She won an Emmy for *The Trial of Mary Lincoln* and the 1985 Memphis Symphony Amphion Award. In the '60s, she spoke to our students on "The Education of the Young Lady of Today, Yesterday, and Tomorrow." Her remarks were interesting and inspiring:

It can be a great adventure ... a continuing adventure ... with ever new challenges and new horizons ... Education must be more than the tool with which we shape our own life. It must be the bridge to reach back and draw from the lives which have gone before us ... and to reach across to the lives which will come after. If there is any way to resolve the conflict between the Chaos and the Conformity of Today, it can be found in the lesson of the Continuity of Man ... the marvelous recurrence of his hopes and dreams ... his failures and his triumphs [and] his cruelties and his sacrifices through the centuries. The shock of recognition that a fact learned in school, is also a happening in real life ... is the great miracle of learning ... and nowhere ... in my experience were facts translated into life terms so well as at St. Mary's.

Although there was a change in ownership and management of St. Mary's at this time, Bishop Gailor continued to have a vital interest in the school. He presided at meetings of the Board of Trustees, had conferences with Helen Loomis and the trustees, and was always present at commencement exercises, giving out the diplomas and delivering the commencement addresses. It was, however, Miss Loomis and Miss Neely who were responsible for carrying

Julia Taylor, Rosa May Clark, and Katherine Brown at commencement, 1925.

out the standards and ideals of the school. According to recollections of alumnae and former teachers, the two of them were an excellent team and responsible for St. Mary's continued success.

Thoughts and anecdotes of alumnae and friends about these principals reveal some of the reasons for the stability and reputation of St. Mary's from 1922-49.

Miss Loomis, a native of Albany, New York, was a graduate of Cornell University, and began her teaching career at St. Mary's in

Miss Loomis in the 1940s.

1897. In trying to discover information about Miss Loomis, Dr. N.C. Hughes, Jr., St. Mary's Headmaster, 1962-73, corresponded with her niece, Helen Hines Rechnitzer of Slingerlands, New York, who could not find any information or records about St. Mary's School, but provided a little background information about Miss Loomis. She was born in Stamford, New York, in the heart of the Catskill Mountains on August 7, 1870. Miss Rechnitzer's letter clearly indicated that education was her heritage, for she remarked that Miss Loomis "was a direct descendant of the Loomis brothers who received a grant from the King of England in the 1600s, consisting of a large tract of land in the Connecticut Valley." They founded a school for boys at Windsor, Connecticut, which, at the time this letter was written, had an excellent reputation.

Wonderful stories are told about Miss Loomis. The memories of her students and her contemporaries give a vivid picture of Miss Loomis as a person and administrator and make me realize the heritage she left the school. In answer to a request for thoughts about her, some interesting and perceptive comments were written by Mary Ann Robertson '44:

> *If faced with finding of one word to best sum up the character of Helen Loomis, I think I would have to settle for "genuine." She was completely without sham or hypocrisy ... With Miss Loomis, you knew where you stood — and you took pains to merit her approval.*

Why did Miss Loomis choose to teach in Memphis? There is no known reference as to how this occurred, but a likely assumption is that it was through a connection with an Episcopal School in New York. Her niece has a slight recollection of her teaching in Peekskill, New York, where the Order of St. Mary, the same Order that sent the Sisters to St. Mary's in Memphis, was in charge of St. Gabriel's School. Conceivably, Miss Loomis could have taught at this school. Her niece's letter contains the information that in the late 1920s she was listed in *Who's Who In America* and also in a publication called *Famous Women of America*.

Mrs. Rechnitzer concluded her letter with the words: "My Aunt Nell was a very remarkable person." This accolade is in total agreement with many of Miss Loomis' former students in Memphis. As alumnae talk about her, their eyes glisten with happy memories, and their voices seem to echo the refrain, "She was a very remarkable person."

Many of her students recall a beautiful, soft voice, coupled with an excellent command of the English language. She was also known as a renowned Latin teacher, as emphasized enthusiastically by Mary Ann Robertson's description:

> Nothing short of your best merited her praise ... Latin as taught by Miss Loomis was far from a "dead language." It made sense because it provided the skeleton on which the English language is built ... Even today—confronted by an unfamiliar word—I can hear Miss Loomis' voice chiding: 'break it down, break it down.' With her love of order and sound thinking, Miss Loomis was a firm believer in diagramming ... Subject, predicate, and adjectives fell neatly into place as she performed an autopsy on a difficult sentence. Even a sentence from Faulkner could be reduced to orderliness under Miss Loomis' scalpel. Today, when in doubt, I find myself mentally drawing a diagram and everything becomes crystal clear.

Nancy Little Oliver '45 remembers, "Miss Loomis made her students keep a list of Latin words that they knew had English derivatives—a wonderful exercise that is still handy today."

Students enjoyed hearing her talk and soon discovered that she had extensive knowledge particularly on the subjects of astronomy and psychology. She inspired her students to read, as another excerpt from Mary Ann Robertson states:

Although she had a "no non-sense" approach to learning, Miss Loomis, according to Ms. Robertson, was also an extremely human person:

Her interests were catholic. She devoured detective novels like peanuts, even though, with her rapier-sharp mind, she must have guessed the murderer after the first page. You could talk to Miss Loomis about anything, because she was interested in everything. Nothing surprised her, and very little could shock her.

Students enjoy the springtime.

Scratch a St. Mary's graduate—and you will almost invariably find an inveterate reader. The caliber of the reading matter may range from Plutarch to Peyton Place—, but, at least, the St. Mary's graduate does read and can differentiate between good and bad writing.

As an experienced teacher, she emphasized it was more important to know where and how to find data than to learn details. Correct pronunciation was "an obsession" with Miss Loomis, not only in English, but also in foreign languages, and speaking like "southern belles" was discouraged daily. She constantly encouraged students to write, and by fourth and fifth grades, they were writing poetry and sonnets. Another requirement was that the hesitation step be absolutely perfect at Commencement. It was practiced endlessly until she was completely satisfied. There is no doubt that she was a perfectionist, for alumnae remember the many, many hours she spent rehearsing the first line of the hymn, "Crown Him with Many Crowns."

Miss Loomis had a distinctive appearance—red hair and a thin, prominent nose that often evoked comments from the students. One alumna described her nose as "magnificent." Another alumna and later a teacher at St. Mary's, Julia Taylor Hughes '25, remarked, "Miss Loomis had a sharp nose that looked like a spear." Many of her students have vivid memories of her dressed fashionably in brightly

colored bouclè suits, in vogue during the 1920s. On that "magnificent nose" resided a pair of gold pince- nez glasses, and she often looked over them to remind the students to remember their "P's and Q's."

Another alumna highlighted her adventuresome spirit. One of the great joys of her life was the possession of a Model T Ford which was seen frequently on the streets of Memphis. She had an accident in this beloved Ford and received a very noticeable black eye—increasing the size of her already large nose. The next day at Chapel, the students could barely contain their laughter, but all managed to do so, except for one student who could not control herself. She was quickly sent from the room, shaking with fear as she awaited her punishment. Miss Loomis left the Chapel, carefully closing the door behind her. Imagine the student's relief when she saw Miss Loomis with a smile on her face and her surprise when Miss Loomis said, "I do look awful and I don't blame you one bit for laughing." This wonderful sense of humor, along with the very human trait of being able to laugh at herself, endeared her to her many students. Nancy Little Oliver '45, revealed another sign of her adventuresome spirit. Before the First World War and prior to the time many women traveled to Europe alone, Miss Loomis courageously took a trip to Italy. She was caught there at exactly the wrong time, and the only way she could return to the States was to go to the United States Embassy for permission. It must have been a very perilous time to travel the Atlantic Ocean but the trip demonstrates that living dangerously was part of her nature.

Miss Loomis was a strict disciplinarian. Her presence in a room immediately demanded respect. Alumnae have mentioned, "Discipline was never a problem in her class and it never left a sting." A favorite remark was, "We don't do that at St. Mary's," and according to several alums, "They didn't." In the early days, no one could wear make-up, and if anyone was suspected of wearing it, she would have to scrub her face immediately. For one alumna, skipping an afternoon at school resulted in a punishment that seemed interminable. The truant was required to stay in Miss Loomis' office to study mathematics, her weakest subject, four hours for every hour missed at school.

Despite this firmness, her understanding of girls and her sympathetic nature are obvious in several alumnae stories. One year a student from Japan moved to Memphis and attended St. Mary's;

homesickness almost overwhelmed her. Miss Loomis, searching for a way to help overcome the homesickness, discovered the student had a dog she dearly loved. In her empathetic way, Miss Loomis suggested she bring her dog, Emmeline, to school. This solution solved the problem for the student and, of course, the dog immediately became a pet of all the other students. Julia Hughes '25 relates another story about a dog, which emphasizes Miss Loomis' keen understanding of her students. These are Julia's words:

> I found a puppy in the street outside the school. It was raining hard and the puppy was soaking wet, consequently I took the puppy into the school and one of the teachers said she would have to put it out for puppies didn't belong in school. Miss Loomis happened to see me and said that it was such a bad day that I would be allowed to keep the puppy in school.

Needless to say, Julia loved Miss Loomis from that day on!

Miss Loomis' insight into handling students is obvious in another story Julia Hughes tells about one of the teachers, Miss Bohmfold, a Northerner. It seems Julia, in answer to a query from Miss Bohmfold, said "Yes ma'am" to her, as she had been instructed. Miss Bohmfold laughed at this Southern idiom. Julia, embarrassed and infuriated, responded with a rude and very unladylike remark for which she was sent to Miss Loomis. According to Julia, Miss Loomis calmed her spirits and suggested she "refrain from rude remarks in the future, but added that she understood her reaction." Many memories recalled and related by alumnae give a clear picture of well-earned love and respect.

Miss Loomis wrote a letter to Bishop Gailor that clearly demonstrates her leadership ability and wisdom in a difficult situation with her faculty. Evidently, several faculty members, unbeknownst to her, were leaving to open another school. According to Bishop Gailor's files, she wrote a letter asking for advice:

> My policy has been to avoid the appearance of panic and I have made no public announcement other than to insert the enclosed advertisement in the papers, and to send the letter out with the applications ... Alumnae and some staunch friends of the school are rising to its defense, but I am trying to hold them from any action beyond quiet statement of our attitude till your arrival ... Their advertisement covers high school.

Teachers under Miss Loomis: Miss Bohmfold, Mrs. Kelly, and Mrs. Anderson.

Letha Cranford Elliott '54 remembers Miss Neely as an extremely fascinating individual and paints a complimentary description of her as an English teacher:

> *She spoke English, as though she had lived in England instead of being a Tennessean. She had the knack of instilling the love of her subject in her pupils and I remember with joy her mythology class. To this day, I have never forgotten the names of the Roman and Greek gods.*

In my conversation with Nancy Little Oliver '45, I discovered she had lived at the school from the time she was in the fifth grade until she graduated from high school. She had many loving recollections of Miss Neely and Miss Loomis. They both gave her a great deal of love and made her life at St. Mary's a happy time. Nancy remembers that Miss Neely was like a mother, sewing on her nametags before she went to camp in the summers and helping her pack her trunk in the fall she left for Vanderbilt. Nancy felt St. Mary's was her home.

Several faculty members did leave, but because of her calmness and the support of her patrons and the Bishop, the school continued to operate successfully.

As mentioned previously, Miss Katherine Neely was Principal of the Lower School from 1922-1949 and worked very closely with Miss Loomis. She was a native of Bolivar, Tennessee, attended Columbia University, and graduated from the University of Pennsylvania as well as the University of Chicago. Although her home was originally in Bolivar, she was an excellent public relations person for St. Mary's, for she had many contacts in Memphis.

Gilmore Lynn, an elementary school teacher during the years Miss Neely was Principal of the Lower School, remembers her "as being a master of the English language, and of having the ability to express herself, both orally and in writing."

Other recollections by Ms. Elliott give additional information about Miss Neely's responsibilities. At this time, the school was both a day and boarding school, and it was Miss Neely's assignment to run the boarding department consisting of girls between the ages of 14-18. This she accomplished efficiently with a "minimum of effort." It was a very proper and formal school, with an emphasis on teaching manners the Victorian way. Students had to form a line to say "hello" to the principal in the morning and also "good-by" as they left in the afternoon. They evidently had to speak to quite a few of the teachers, for Ms. Elliott recalls the French teacher always saying, "Au Revoir, Ma Petite." Tea was served in the Big House, where the boarders lived and where attendance was obligatory on fairly frequent occasions. Students were required to sit with their backbones rigid and to hold a teacup formally. At the time, according to Ms. Elliott, "We dreaded these teas, but as I look back and think about them now, the memory gives me a very warm feeling." Mrs. Lynn also remembers that teaching the students the social graces was a part of Miss Neely's assigned responsibilities, and thought a suitable nickname for her might be "Miss Manners."

Ms. Elliott recalls an unusual mathematics teacher who would not ignore any mistake a student made. For each mistake, instead of simply correcting her, she threw a thimbleful of water at the student. Drama was Elliott's favorite activity which took place in the attic, hence the name "The Attic Players." This was the beginning of Ms.

Elliott's love of acting, which is still very important to her. Today, she enjoys being a part of the Memphis drama community.

Much emphasis during these years was placed on the arts, and times were scheduled for ballet, music, and art appreciation. This was the era in which Walter Damrosch, chorus master of the Metropolitan Opera House, taught music appreciation over the radio every Saturday afternoon, and the students were required to listen. From 1942-1949, "Dancing on the Green," one of their favorite activities, was taught by Mary Walton Glass, a well- known Memphis

Dance teacher Henrietta S. Strickland.

Court of St. Mary's 1930: (left to right) Charlotte Berlin, Florence Wilson, Anne Brown Taylor, Alice McKee, Mary Jane Stimpson, Jane Buck, and Elizabeth Harvey.

ballet teacher. Traditions initiated during the era of the Sisters were carried on by faculty and students during the Loomis/Neely years, one of the most anticipated being May Day. Our earliest written account of a May Day is in 1922, when the school was located on Poplar.

The queen's court processed on the green and was preceded by the entire student body, dressed in fancy costumes, marching to the strains of an orchestra, and kneeling as the queen passed by. The queen wore a long white dress decorated with pearls and ermine. It was the custom for the retiring queen to place the crown on the new queen's head, a symbol of her high office.

Another tradition that came alive again in 1925 was a school newspaper called *The Tatler*, which was similar in form to the 1903 one. It contains an article entitled "A Friendly Comment," which includes the following paragraph:

My Dear Tatler: That you have risen, a Phoenix, after your ashes were cold and dull, is a surpassing of the miraculous bird's best achievement. The old Saint Mary's *Tatler* has been 'decently interred these many years.' Whatever has quickened it into life again deserves acclaim for the lustiness of its creation. The first number is a good one and I, for my part, send wishes for a long and vigorous new life.

The Magazine Board, as it was called at that time, included the following members: Editor-in-Chief, Catherine Underwood; Associate Editors: Fay Hines, Barbara Embury, Katherine Lockwood, Elizabeth Patterson, Louise Miller, Valerie Ganong, Nancy Schutter, Rosa May Clark. Business Managers were Beatrice Scheibler, Secretary, and Julia Taylor, Treasurer.

An article by Zona Bond gives some insight into the arrival of spring while St. Mary's was located at 1257 Poplar:

It is spring at St. Mary's. Merry ripples of laughter and the chirping of birds float through the well loved grounds. One sure sign is that chapel comes the first thing in the morning, and instead of voices quavering with the cold, feebly singing the familiar hymns, they now ring out glad and clear. A few have the privilege of studying out of doors alone, and the others go in groups chaperoned by the teachers. The latters' desks are adorned with every kind of lovely flowers obtainable; we know the way to teachers' hearts. 'Hurrah, we dance outdoors tomorrow.' At three o'clock the playground teacher comes and the Primary and Elementary departments roll about like so many Easter eggs, making a sight so pretty that proud mothers park their cars and wait without grumbling until the game is finished. The tennis courts are nearly finished … The days are longer and we have more time for the enchanting out of door things.

During these years, another tradition was added—the English essay composition. On an unannounced date, Miss Loomis would say: "This is the day for the English essay competition." Five titles would be written on the blackboard; the students were asked to select one. First, the essay was to be written in pencil, then carefully copied in ink in manuscript writing. An award was given for the best

An article in St. Mary's archives tells about different schools in Memphis— Southwestern, Lausanne, Miss Hutchison's, St. Mary's— "Rallying to British Relief." The word is that ... knitting needles are going to set the style for Memphis' young people this year ... St. Mary's Episcopal School has gone in for the project whole-heartedly ... Even the Kindergarten group will take part. Very young Catherine Meacham, Kindergarten student, will talk to her class about their helping ... [and] Irene McDonnell is St. Mary's senior class chairman." Others working on this project are Helen Shawhan, Barbara Lowe, Carolyn Sanders, Margaret Loaring-Clark, Grace Marie Hall, Joan Manley, Mimi Gardner, Norma Shelton, and Lura Mundy.

essay. This competition was revived during the sixties in honor of both Miss Loomis and Miss Neely by Nancy Little Oliver '45. It is still in existence, and the essays are judged by a Rhodes College professor. The school is in debt to Mrs. Oliver for providing books for the winners in each division of the school.

Probably St. Mary's most beloved tradition is the Christmas Pageant, which has been in existence over 100 years. It began during the years the Sisters were operating the school, but there is no clear documentation about it during those years. When the school was located next door to the original Cathedral, the Pageant was performed in the small wooden Chapel. It was an elaborate production requiring many hours of work after school and into the night. After the completion of the present Cathedral, the arches on either side of the chancel in St. Mary's Cathedral served as frames for the living pictures—usually five or six portrayals of famous portraits of the life of Christ.

Within each arch, a stage was built several feet above floor level and electrical fixtures were arranged for proper lighting. Girls who were not in the portraits sang in the choir. Each portrait had its own special song, and other carols were sung between portraits.

Although the school moved to 1257 Poplar in 1923, the Pageant continued to be at the Cathedral until the early 1930s. At that time, the decision was made to move the performance to the attic. It was still elaborately performed, but production there proved much easier because stage, lighting, and curtains were permanent.

St. Mary's remained at this location on Poplar with Helen Loomis and Katherine Neely as Principals until 1949. Miss Loomis announced her retirement at a meeting held on February 8, 1949. Bishop Dandridge, the successor to Bishop Maxon, and Dr. Theodore Nott Barth, Bishop Coadjutor, held a conference about continuing the school. The result was that "they encountered considerable agitation about the future of St. Mary's School, Memphis."

During these Loomis/Neely years, there were many obstacles in the way of running a successful independent school such as St. Mary's. The remarkable fact is the school survived under their competent leadership despite two World Wars and the Great Depression. Unfortunately, they could not find a buyer for the school in 1949. Although the school had continued to be successful under Miss Loomis and Miss Neely, there could have been several reasons for this lack of interest in purchasing the school. One reason could be

Commencement, 1947.

that the location was becoming less advantageous. Memphis was growing towards the east, and, according to Sigafoos, "The majority of single family homes were in East Memphis sub-divisions beyond the Parkway System." Another reason may have been because there was more competition from other independent schools: Miss Hutchison School opened in 1902, Lausanne School in 1926, and the many Catholic Schools. They all operated for the same purpose—the education of girls. Central High was known as an outstanding high school, and East High was being built to accommodate students whose families were moving eastward. All these circumstances could have been deterrents to the ownership of St. Mary's.

This letter was written to Miss Loomis by Charles E. Diehl, President of Southwestern University:

This is to state that the graduates of St. Mary's School are accepted at Southwestern by certificate and that they are cordially welcomed among our student body. The students whom we have received from St. Mary's School have been among our very best students. By the high rank which they have taken in their classes they have evidenced the fact that their preparation was thorough, and by their interest and attitude towards college duties and activities they have shown that their preparation was well rounded. The emphasis which is laid at St. Mary's on morals and manners, as well as on sound learning, is in accord with our own principles and ideals.

Commencement 1949 was the last formal activity of the school on Poplar Avenue. After Miss Loomis sold the school property, she moved to Albany, New York, to live with her sister, and Miss Neely accepted a position at Miss Hutchison's School to teach English and drama in the elementary department.

The *Memphis Press/Scimitar* published the following about the closing of the Upper School with the good news that the Lower School would continue:

Historic St. Mary's School ... which has been attended by daughters and granddaughters of some of Memphis' most promising families will not re-open this fall.

Miss Katherine Neely and Miss Helen A. Loomis, co- directors of the school, announced today that it had been found impossible to continue the school, since its properties must be sold in order to dissolve the partnership under which they have operated ...

In recent years the school has prospered, with an enrollment of about two hundred. It has played a major part in Memphis' social and cultural development ...

Miss Neely said, 'We deeply regret that the school must be closed, but it is the only way in which our partnership can be properly dissolved.'

In September of 1949, there was another announcement in the *Press/Scimitar* about the opening of the school:

"St. Mary's School to Reopen Grades"

Historic St. Mary's Episcopal School will reopen with the first through the fourth grades and a Kindergarten at Grace-St. Luke's Episcopal Church, under the leadership of Mrs. John R. Lynn and Mrs. A.D. Parker. The Kindergarten under the direction of Mrs. Griffin Walker, assisted by Mrs. Hugh Lawless, Jr., and Mrs. May Frances McDermott, will open on Monday, September 19. Mrs. Percy Glass, the former Mary Walton Soihm, will be associated with the school as a dance instructor.

Although St. Mary's was forced to move to another location and was a much smaller school, the spirit of St. Mary's simply refused to die. At this very difficult time, the school demonstrated its character and courage, climbing to new successes under the guiding and capable hands of Gilmore Lynn.

4. DREAMS AND DETERMINATION

Gilmore Lynn

From the very first day I arrived at St. Mary's, I knew I would enjoy working with Gilmore Lynn. My previous experience in Memphis had been at a rival girls' school where I often heard of her reputation as an outstanding educator. After arriving at St. Mary's, I discovered the truth of this statement in a very short time. She was not only a fine teacher and administrator, but also a wise counselor. Her wisdom and devotion to the school had a profound influence on me. I admired her especially for never wavering from her insistence on high scholastic and ethical standards for her students and the school.

Gilmore Bicknell Lynn, teacher 1943-1975; principal 1949-1971.

Gilmore Lynn's years as Principal of St. Mary's occurred at the time of a rapid population growth in Memphis, following World II. The city doubled its size during the next generation. After many years of being in political control, the Crump machine was losing its power, and real change was occurring in the government of Memphis. There was a rapid turnover of mayors from Watkins Overton elected in 1951 to Frank Tobey in 1953, to Edmund Orgill in 1955. An entirely new city was born: the Memphis/Arkansas bridge was built; many new areas were developed; the first Holiday Inn opened in 1952; the Memphis Belle, a B-17 bomber which had made many successful raids over Germany during World War II was returned to Memphis; W.C. Handy and Elvis Presley brought musical fame to the city. World War II opened many opportunities for women to work at plants; women also drove buses and streetcars for the Memphis Street Railway and were employed by the government. This era began a time of enormous change for women. The world was beginning to appreciate women for their brains, not just for their home and social skills.

Likewise, St. Mary's School in 1949 was undergoing a tremendous transition. Although it had become a smaller school with only four grades, it had managed to survive. The Upper and Middle grades of the school were closed, and St. Mary's had a new Principal, Mrs. Gilmore Lynn. The school moved to a new location; the size was reduced and it became a day school only. It seemed that just as Memphis was moving forward, the heyday of St. Mary's was over. Could it be that this school with all its changes could again develop into twelve grades? To anyone who knew Mrs. Lynn, anything was possible.

Gilmore Lynn first became associated with St. Mary's School in 1943 through the recommendation of Miriam Herstein Kelly, a teacher at St. Mary's for many years. Her career began by teaching first and second grades together in the same room. In her book, *History of St. Mary's School 1943-1975*, she tells of many happy moments teaching under Miss Loomis and Miss Neely. Her first year revealed the creative way she handled challenges:

> The second grade started a week early so that a regular morning program could be planned to keep that grade busy when the first grade arrived. More attention could be given to first graders, who needed individual assistance during the period of adjustment.

It did not seem difficult for her to have the two grades in one room, for both grades were taught the same subjects: writing, phonics, art, ballet, and French. In her words, "review was good for second graders." During the years 1943-1949, she continued her teaching in first and second grades and became known as an unusually fine elementary school teacher.

Miss Loomis' and Miss Neely's decision to retire and sell the school and its property in 1949 presented a difficult decision for Mrs. Lynn. They both encouraged her to continue St. Mary's by including as many grades as possible. It was a serious undertaking and a big responsibility, but Mrs. Lynn, after much prayer, thought, and planning, decided to accept the challenge. Her plan and hope was to begin with the primary grades (1-4) and to add a grade a year as space allowed. Amazingly, Mrs. Lynn, along with Mrs. A.D. Parker, another elementary school teacher, became responsible for the very survival of St. Mary's School. Mrs. Griffin Walker, a Kindergarten teacher at Grace St. Luke's, suggested that Mrs. Lynn talk to Dr. Charles S. Hale, Rector of Grace-St. Luke's Church, about holding classes at the same location. The school opened there with four grades in the fall of 1949. The first year they were very limited in space—one basement room, one room on the first floor, and another on the second. The rooms were separated by plastic dividers, which made it possible to have six classrooms. The school was small, but it was a beginning. Mrs. Lynn was delighted to have a roof over their heads and characteristically she took whatever was available and made the best of it.

Miss Loomis had mentioned to Mrs. Lynn her desire for her to have the school's desks. As she gave these desks to her, Mrs. Lynn remembers Miss Loomis emphasizing that "they were her very special gift for her to use." Before moving them, it was obvious they needed refinishing. It proved to be quite an undertaking, as described in the following words:

> Armed with strong soap, stiff brushes and varnish remover, we enlisted all the family members available and willing; and went to work. We scraped, scrubbed and sanded every desk. Then we applied shellac ... Those sturdy old desks of solid cherry and solid oak were beautiful antiques to us.

As a consequence of all this work, they needed to buy very little furniture. John Lynn, her husband, was instrumental in the

Mrs. A.D. Parker, Lower School Assistant Principal.

Allyson Patterson, class of 2011, enjoys one of the original school desks, a gift from Helen Loomis to Gilmore Lynn, refinished by her husband.

St. Mary's at Grace-St. Luke's.

refurbishing process. He remarked, "Every student in the forties must have had a penknife!" These desks were used both at Grace-St. Luke's and later at the Church of the Holy Communion.

The church cafeteria at Grace-St. Luke's was not available for the school, but the refrigerator was used for storing the daily supply of milk. Home-made soup, made and brought by Mrs. Lynn in large thermos jugs, was lunch four days a week, and spaghetti, a special dish on the fifth day, was reheated on a small heater which was actually provided to give warmth for the first grade room. There was no office, nor was there any space to have one. Outside the class-room on the first floor, there was a telephone, an unabridged dictionary, and a set of *Compton's Encyclopedias.* According to Mrs. Lynn, "that was their library." A playground, across the street from the church and already in existence, was used daily by the students.

Gilmore Lynn, a superior teacher, was more interested in teaching than in administrative work. Her love of the school, how-ever, and her eagerness to have St. Mary's continue, made it necessary for her to become an administrator, a position for which she was highly qualified, if not by her desire, certainly by her knowl-edge, ability, and gracious manner. Several teachers came with her to Grace-St. Luke's: Mrs. Parker, Assistant Principal, Mrs. Quincy Wolf, choral singing, and Miss Elizabeth Mosby, private piano lessons.

French was taught the first year by the many-faceted Mrs. Lynn, who had experience teaching this language in another school. But, enough was enough—the second year she asked Miss Janine Gontard to join the faculty to teach French. Tuition for the first year was $125 for the first grade and $225 for the second through the fourth grades. The enrollment the first year consisted of Grade 1, 27 pupils (17 girls, 10 boys); Grade 2 (15 girls); Grade 3 (14 girls); Grade 4 (4 girls); totaling 60. Mrs. Lynn taught the first grade in the morning and Mrs. Parker and Mrs. Metcalf, the second and third grades all day; Mrs. Lynn worked with them part time in the afternoon. It was indeed a busy time. After teaching a full day, she undertook the administrative work which occupied most of her time in the late afternoons and evenings.

Evidently Miss Loomis was worried about continuing the name of the school, for in 1951, she wrote a letter to Mrs. Lynn advising her to have a legal document stating that Mrs. Lynn's St. Mary's School was the former St. Mary's Episcopal School. Mrs. Lynn had no idea of changing the name of the school, but Miss Loomis was concerned that someone else might be interested in opening a school with St. Mary's name unless there were a binding contract. This letter details Miss Loomis's concern. Mrs. Lynn consulted a lawyer who felt there was no problem, since St. Mary's had been incorporated when it moved from the church property to 1257 Poplar.

Mrs. Lynn was determined to continue the Christmas Pageant. However, it was a very different performance, since the school had only four grades. One of the teachers, Mrs. Pat Fentress, found a

The Christmas Pageant at Grace-St. Luke's.

large gold frame made at the Art Academy, and Mr. John Lynn, Mrs. Lynn's husband, made supports for the frame and created a box-like setting for the tableaux. Mrs. Quincy Wolfe trained the choir of little girls and first grade boys.

The result was a beautiful and inspiring pageant. This box, redesigned by Mr. Lynn, is still in existence, and Mrs. Lynn's son built the electrical box from which the lights are operated. In recent years, the students who have attended St. Mary's for twelve years are the participants in the tableaux. The second and third grades from the Lower School accompany the pictures with appropriate songs. It is a moving and spiritual experience to observe these living tableaux and to hear the joyful voices of the little children.

The first "graduation" from this new school, consisting of sixth graders, was in 1952. Unfortunately, there was no room to add another grade. Mrs. Lynn searched for a new location, which would provide more space, and talked with the Reverend Eric Greenwood, Rector, about the possibility of moving the school to the Church of the Holy Communion. He was interested, but could not give a definitive answer. No agreement had been reached as to the exact date for the completion of the church educational building under construction. This building would be necessary to provide enough room for the school. Following its completion in 1953, George Phillips, a member of the Church of the Holy Communion, contacted Mrs. Lynn about her desire to move the school. She was invited to talk to the Vestry. They were so impressed with her and her plans for St. Mary's that the Vestry presented the idea to the congregation, which agreed, but only if the school did not get in the way of the church. Mrs. Lynn's decision to move was also influenced by the prediction of city planners, who believed this corner of Walnut Grove and Perkins Extended would soon become a central location in Memphis.

During the month of July 1953, the move was made to Holy Communion Church. Although the new facility provided the much-needed space, difficulties remained. They were within the city limits, but very few deliveries were made that far east. Everything except milk had to be delivered to Mrs. Lynn's home on Auburndale and brought to the school in her car. One alumna remembers Mrs. Lynn opening the trunk of the car every morning and bringing in numerous supplies—including food for lunch which she had prepared the previous evening.

In 1953, an article in the Press/Scimitar *describes the move of St. Mary's to the Church of the Holy Communion (pictured right):*

> *St. Mary's Episcopal School for Girls will open at a new location in September, Mrs. John R. Lynn, principal, announced today.*
>
> *The church school will find a new home at the Church of the Holy Communion … Now located at Grace-St. Luke's Episcopal Church, the school will move its six grades into a new administration building with 20 acres of ground at the new location. Mrs. Lynn said the facilities at the Church of the Holy Communion offer what she hopes will be a permanent home for the school.*

Church of the Holy Communion

There were many requests for Mrs. Lynn to open a Kindergarten. Two problems existed: no money and very little furniture. Again, Mr. Lynn came to her rescue. He volunteered to build some of the necessary furniture which made it possible to open the Kindergarten. Seventy-nine students came from Grace-St. Luke's with Mrs. Lynn. Adding a Kindergarten of 45 boys and girls made the first year at Holy Communion total 144 students. For several years, St. Mary's was actually co-educational. Boys continued to attend St. Mary's through the third grade, but in 1956, it was decided by the Board of Trustees to limit the school to girls as it had been originally. In 1956, the anticipated plan to add a grade a year had to be postponed for a year as the school had grown rapidly, and there was no room for a seventh grade. Seeing the need for more room, George Phillips, Chairman of the Board of Trustees, influenced the vestry to allow the school use of the "White House" in back of the church for classes; it contained a very large room suitable for division. Once more, Mr. Lynn resolved the problem by making portable dividers for the different grades. At the end of the each week, these were removed, and the room was prepared for the church Sunday school.

As there was no space for a real library, Mrs. Lynn again found a way to manage. The Memphis Public Library had a plan to deliver books each month to the County schools and, at Mrs. Lynn's request, began bringing books to St. Mary's.

Mrs. Lynn reading to Sally Fri, class of 1974.

Mrs. Lynn with her first grade class.

Each month, we received twenty-five books for each grade first through sixth ... Each room had a private library ... and all the transporting was done by the library. We were learning that our remoteness was not too far for the library or the milkman!

The church kitchen and dining room were available for the school's use. The playground was improved by the grandfather of one of St. Mary's students. Finally the school had an office, a small enclosed space on the second floor which gave a modicum of privacy.

Day by day, the school grew. By 1957, the enrollment was 239 pupils with 17 faculty members. A charter and by-laws were drawn and the school became incorporated under the laws of the State of Tennessee for the following general purposes:

Educational, scientific and literary purposes for the general welfare.

To own, operate and conduct a secondary school or preparatory school for university or college education.

To establish and provide an institution with a Christian and American background.

To continue and carry forward St. Mary's Episcopal School which was founded in Memphis, Tennessee.

The Commercial Appeal *article announces the church's plan to expand, which will also allow more room for St. Mary's School:*

A $700,000 program to expand the Church of the Holy Communion and St. Mary's Episcopal School was unfolded before communicants last night. William L. Quinlen, Jr., general chairman of the building fund campaign, said tentative plans are to add an administrative wing to the church... lengthen the nave, add two wings to the educational building and erect a combination auditorium-gymnasium... The additions will be primarily for the church and Sunday school, although St. Mary's will benefit.

During these years, Mrs. Lynn and Mrs. Parker managed all the secretarial work and the bookkeeping with the help of a CPA. According to Mrs. Lynn, the survival of the school was due to the dedication and the enthusiastic support of both teachers and friends who were willing and eager to give of their talents and time.

The Church, as well as the school, was growing tremendously, and more room was needed. The church decided to erect another building, which was named Greenwood for the Rector of the Church of the Holy Communion. Construction continued throughout the school year. As Mrs. Lynn mentioned, "It was a noisy time for students and teachers, but thinking of the space it would provide, we tried hard to regard it as music to our ears." In this new building, it would be possible to have several classrooms, a library, and a small science room.

Louise Rooke, ballet teacher from 1954-1985, taught every class, culminating in a beautiful May Day performance each year. The following year, 1958-1959, some of the rooms were still not ready to be used, and as a result, there was no adequate space for ballet. Derek Rooke, Louise's husband, offered to make the rooms suitable for ballet. He bought heavy plywood and smooth flooring to place on the concrete floors. Bars were added to the unfinished walls, but alas, there were no mirrors. Mrs. Lynn remarked, "the little girls just

Ballet dancers ready for May Day.

Stella Moody, a special friend to all the students. Anyone who was at St. Mary's in the 1950s and 1960s knew and loved Stella Moody, a member of the maintenance staff. As Mrs. Lynn remarked, "Without the help of Stella Moody, I could not have continued St. Mary's." Stella took care of Mrs. Lynn's mother during her nine years' illness and never missed a day at work. When Mrs. Lynn's mother died in 1954, she began her work at St. Mary's and only missed two days during her many years at the school. That was when her own mother died. She was a friend and confidante to the students, and alumnae remember her with affection and high regard.

couldn't see how gracefully they danced. It is surprising what we can do without, if necessary."

It was Mrs. Lynn's decision that she could no longer teach first grade and also head the school, As a result of her decision, St. Mary's had its first Headmaster, Mr. Lawrence Lobaugh, who began his years at St. Mary's in 1958. Mrs. Lynn remained as Principal of the Lower School, first through sixth, and continued teaching first grade. As first grade attended school only from 8:45-12:00 noon, her afternoons were free for overseeing other grades, for parent conferences, and for all the other myriad details of a school principal.

The 1984 fall issue of *St. Mary's News* praised Mrs. Lynn as being "a master teacher and a remarkable educator." But, before she came to St. Mary's School in 1943, she had been forced to resign from the public school system, due to its regulation that "only men or single women, unmarried or widowed, may teach in the school system." When she was married in 1929, her termination was automatic. This regulation, insulting and degrading to women, was St. Mary's good fortune. The school was in need of her enterprise, energy, unfailing sense of humor, and her determination.

In addition to being Principal and teaching first grade, she spent time encouraging her faculty, reassuring and counseling young parents, handling all the business operations, and running a delivery service. Her school was a beehive of activity. The "wilderness" surrounding St. Mary's at that time resulted in wonderful opportunities for challenging Easter Egg Hunts and daily nature study. After a teacher discovered a snake in the building, however, Gilmore accepted a grandfather's offer to trim the adjacent meadows. Each year, a grade was added, and tuition increased $5.

Mrs. Lynn's love was teaching children, and she was a master. Her presence at St. Mary's insured that the high moral, spiritual, and academic standards of the original school were never diluted. One of the teachers tells the story of a little girl who had taken something valuable from another student's desk which, after questioning, she refused to admit.

Mrs. Lynn had a conference with the student's mother telling her about the incident: "Your daughter has stolen something valuable from another student and will not admit it. I want her to understand that she has stolen it and must return it with an apology." The mother replied, "The girl was too young to have the word, stolen,

Mrs. Lynn and students in the breezeway.

used about her and couldn't Mrs. Lynn use another softer expression such as borrowed or took." Mrs. Lynn responded: "We need to deal with this now and not water it down." The mother, realizing Mrs. Lynn's love and concern for her students and their moral behavior, accepted this counseling with gratitude.

In my interview with Nancy Whitman Manire '64, she mentioned that rarely, if ever, did she misbehave in Mrs. Lynn's classroom. She always wanted to please her. Her sister, however, frequently received a red check and her name on the board for talking. After the third red check, her mother questioned why she talked so much. Her response was surprising: "Mrs. Lynn's handwriting is so pretty, I like to see her write my name on the board." It is easy to understand such a woman's influence on the character of the students she taught; she was a person of high morals and demanded high standards of behavior from her girls and her teachers. These are a few of the remarks she shared with her teachers: "Difficulties are opportunities." "Success is nothing but good ideas coupled with hard work." "Keep your fears to yourself. Share your courage with others."

Mrs. Lynn continued as Lower School Principal and first grade teacher until 1971. On account of her health, it became necessary for her to give up her responsibilities as Principal, but she remained as first grade teacher. To the regret of all of us, she resigned in 1975 and was given the honorary title of Principal Emeritus. Dr. Hughes, Headmaster 1962-1973, wrote a beautiful tribute to Mrs. Lynn for her book, *History of St. Mary's, 1943-1975*:

> Four individuals can be said to have been indispensable in the one hundred and fifty year life of St. Mary's School. Mary E. Foote Pope founded the school and guided it through the Civil War years. Sister Hughetta led St. Mary's sadly weakened by the destructive yellow fever epidemic of 1878, into the Twentieth century, and helped make it a stronger institution with a clear sense of mission. Helen A. Loomis took control in 1910 when the sisters withdrew from the charge of St. Mary's School, Memphis, until her retirement in 1949, at which time she sold the school property but transferred the name of St. Mary's and responsibility for its destiny to Mrs. John R. Lynn who had been one of Miss Loomis' teachers.
>
> Gilmore Bicknell Lynn kept St. Mary's alive. She found a temporary home at Grace-St. Luke's Episcopal Church and remained four years until 'no more pupils could be accommodated' in the facilities. She then made an agreement with the Church of the Holy Communion and brought seventy-nine of her students to 4645 Walnut Grove Road in the fall of 1953. And there St. Mary's flourished ... It is a story of faith and perseverance and loyalty, a story worthy of Helen Loomis, Sister Hughetta, and Mary Pope.
>
> There would be no St. Mary's without Gilmore Lynn.
>
> As Principal Emeritus, she is a reminder of the high academic, moral, and spiritual character of St. Mary's, a heritage handed down to her and apparent today because of her dedication to the school.

Katharine Phillips

A school is are greatly influenced by the caliber of the people who involve themselves in its life. As I think about Katharine and George Phillips' years at St. Mary's, I realize the huge debt that the school owes them. Their deep spiritual faith, their devotion to the school, along with their solid support gives me a deeper understanding of the reason for the continued existence of this school. Ever since I began working on this story, I marvel that in every key moment, there have been individuals connected with the school who have envisioned what the school could be and been willing to work towards achieving it.

One of Katharine's wonderful traits was her willingness to step in whenever a need arose. At the time of Helen Allen's resignation as Principal in 1963, Katharine showed this characteristic by taking over the position of Acting Principal for the spring of 1964. On account of the development and growth of the Lower School, Mrs. Lynn needed to be relieved of some of her responsibility. Katharine was asked to be Assistant Principal in 1969; at Mrs. Lynn's retirement in 1975, she was appointed Principal of the Lower School. At that time, St. Mary's was in three divisions—Kindergarten, grades one through six, and grades seven through twelve. When the Moss Hall property became available in 1976, Kindergarten and grades 1-3 moved to this new property with Katharine as its Principal, where she remained until her retirement in 1981.

Katharine first became professionally involved in St. Mary's after it moved to the Church of the Holy Communion. Now, she was not only a parent and a strong supporter, but also a teacher. Mrs. Lynn realized Katharine's talent as a gifted Bible teacher and asked her to teach a Bible class one hour a week. As grades were added and the enrollment increased, more Bible classes and more and more responsibilities were delegated to her. One alumna reminisced that these Bible stories and their characters came alive for her because of Mrs. Phillips' enthusiastic presentation. Katharine frequently ended a story with the remark, "You'll never guess what happened next," leaving the student eager for the following installment.

Mrs. Phillips was not only a student of the Bible, but also a librarian, having earned her degree in library science from Louisiana State University. She agreed to start building a library for the school, but accomplished this in a rather unconventional manner. No money

When the school was located at Grace-St. Luke's, Katharine and George Phillips' daughter, Katharine, was a student there. They were so impressed with Gilmore Lynn, Katharine's teacher, that they encouraged her to move St. Mary's to its present location, the Church of the Holy Communion. They, along with Mrs. Lynn, had a vision that this school would become fully accredited from Kindergarten through the twelfth grade. In this rapidly expanding area east of the city, the school would have more space and opportunity for growth. Without their influence and encouragement, it is doubtful that St. Mary's would have realized this dream.

*Katharine Phillips, Acting Dean,
Upper School, spring 1964, with
students Betty Coe Cruzen '70,
Jean Phillips '69, and Stephanie
Sousoulas '73.*

being available to finance the necessary number of books for state accreditation, she combed her bookcases and her attic and asked her neighbors and friends to do the same. The story is told that she and some of her students worked all night putting pockets in the books until they finally attained the number required by the visiting committee arriving the next day. As the library grew, one by one her books were returned to her, and occasionally, even now, she will find one in her bookcase with a St. Mary's library pocket. Now that the school had a real library, she organized a library club which was very popular and a real service to the school. The students helped shelve the books and check them in and out. At this time, the services of the Public Library, which had been a life-saver, were discontinued with gratitude for their years of tremendous help.

Katharine's job description might include "public relations director" and "college counselor." Because of her enthusiastic advertising of the school's excellent academic curriculum and fine students, St. Mary's began to be recognized in college circles. Her initiative and energy seemed endless. She actually drove a student to Emory University to talk with the Admissions Committee, even though they had previously turned down the student's application. The college was so impressed with this particular student's personality and her obvious academic training that they accepted her immediately.

During the sixties, students were accepted at such prestigious colleges as Wellesley, Radcliffe, Smith, Swarthmore, and Vanderbilt, in addition to many others. Katharine had still another title, not quite as intellectually demanding, but perhaps more nerve-wracking. She filled the very needed position of school chauffeur. One year she

Katharine Phillips, Lower School Principal, with students (left to right) Katie Morris, Debbie Beasley, and Courtney Morris.

Katharine Phillips, librarian, with Jean Phillips '69, Suzanne Brescia '67, Jackie Hill '67, and Ann Gordon '68.

In the early days, initiation lasted one week and was held at the home of one of the senior students. Katharine, along with Helen Allen and the other teachers, was always there to cheer and comfort the freshmen during this rite of passage; they even spent the night. Katharine understood the students' need to have fun along with hard work, and her amazing energy made it into a successful and eventful week, if not entirely for the teachers, certainly for the students.

drove 16 girls from Audubon to Goodlett to Pleasant Acres to St. Mary's, although not all at the same time.

As Katharine talks about St. Mary's, her love and interest in the school is immediately obvious. Foremost among her memories is chapel, which was first held in the church office where there was a fireplace, then in the Children's Chapel, and, as the school grew, the service was promoted to the church. All the students from 1st through 12th grade were a part of the chapel service, thus forming a community of students and faculty who knew and felt at home with each other. Another memory is Freshmen Initiation, initiated by Helen Allen, Principal. During the school's early years, several students reaching the ninth grade wanted to transfer to a public school where there were boys and also sororities. There was no possible way to be co-educational, but the school felt it could reduce this attrition by adding more fun and excitement to the ninth grade, giving the freshmen an opportunity to bond with the seniors. And so began a treasured tradition of the school.

One of Katharine's comments about St. Mary's was that "every teacher who taught at the school did it for one reason only—and that was for her love of teaching. Each one did a little bit of everything; the lines of responsibility were unending." With this attitude on the part of the faculty and administration, it is no wonder that St. Mary's continued to grow and to flourish.

The imprint of Katharine Phillips' character and faith is still felt. She served the school for twenty-four years as a wise counselor to hundreds of girls and their families. In answer to her letter of resignation, the Reverend David Leech, Headmaster (1974-1981), wrote "No one at St. Mary's has borne a heavier load more conscientiously, more gracefully, or longer than has Katharine Phillips." This is a statement echoed by all who worked with her or were taught by her. By her very presence and gracious manner, she instilled love and respect. Her deep religious faith was evident not only in her Bible classes, but also in her daily life, and especially in her relationships with students and members of the faculty and administration. She was a cheerleader for the school as was shown by her constant enthusiasm and unwavering support. Because of her love and service, she was given the title of Principal Emeritus upon her retirement.

The Reverend David Leech, Katharine Phillips, and husband George, at her retirement party, May 1981.

While Katharine's importance to St. Mary's cannot be overestimated, it needs to be mentioned that her husband, George, was also crucial to the growth and survival of the school. We are reminded of this by the following memorial article written by Dr. N.C. Hughes, Jr., Headmaster, at the time of George Phillips' death in 1978:

George Phillips was a hard working member of the Board of Trustees from 1953-1974 and Chairman of the Board of

George Pilkington Phillips, first
Chairman of St. Mary's Board
of Trustees.

Trustees from 1953-1962. He strongly influenced the school's move from Grace-St. Luke's to the Church of the Holy Communion. It was Phillips who had the imagination and faith to see the St. Mary's of today in a tiny group of students and teachers operating in the basement of Grace-St. Luke's. He always saw problems as opportunities and his persuasiveness time and time again turned pessimism into constructive effort ... Perhaps no trustee of St. Mary's has held the respect for integrity and pureness of motive that George enjoyed. George Phillips loved St. Mary's deeply. Nearly every aspect of her rich life owes some obligation to him. He sustained his contributions for a generation because George wanted girls to have the chance to become what they were capable of becoming.

Katharine and George's hopes for the school, combined with their dedication to the accomplishment of these goals, challenges the school of today to remember that dreams can be realized.

Mignon Payne

Mignon Payne, Director of the Kindergarten, was my solid supporter during the year I was Acting Headmistress. She ran the Kindergarten efficiently, never needing any advice or help from me, but every time she realized I had a problem or did not know which way to turn, she was there to offer me her invaluable counsel. Her sudden death in the fall of 1974 was a sad moment for the school and for me personally. She is still vividly alive in the memory of all of us who worked with her and loved her.

Mignon graduated from Messick High School in 1933, and attended Memphis State from 1933-1935. Her first working position was with the Memphis Park Commission as Director of the Community Center and Playgrounds from 1934-1944. During these years, she taught physical education and coached volleyball, drill teams, marching, tumbling, handicraft, and dancing. From 1949-1956, she was employed at Springdale Elementary School as lead teacher and Associate Director. Mignon was one of a group of teachers who started the Memphis Kindergarten Group; she was also an active member in both the Tennessee and the Southern Association for Children Under Six and the National Association for the Education of Young Children.

*Mignon Payne, Kindergarten
Director 1956-1974.*

Mignon's first year as Director of the Kindergarten at St. Mary's
began in the fall of 1956. During her first years here, both boys and
girls were enrolled in the school. Under her leadership, the
Kindergarten had a most successful program, one which was very
much in demand. It was so popular that they had both morning and
afternoon sessions. Along with Mignon, Julia Hughes, Maxine
Stevens, Sydney Bates, Betty Lyon, and Sue Williams were among the
teachers responsible for its success. A "graduation" program was initiated by the Kindergarten teachers in which all the students
performed. The Mother's Club made mortar boards and capes for the
children, and each child was given a special diploma presented by
the Headmaster. Under Mignon's guidance, the teachers designed
and made costumes (some of which are still in use today). They

Kindergarten graduation program.

choreographed dances, even with hoops and bouncing balls; they learned poems and songs until, as one teacher remembered, "we felt like we had a Broadway production." Every Kindergarten student was involved, resulting in hundreds of parents and grandparents attending the program. It proved to be a most successful public relations event for the school.

One of the teachers, who worked with Mignon many years, revealed one of the many reasons she was a successful administrator. Mignon was a talented pianist, while this teacher could only "play" with one hand and was embarrassed as she heard Mignon playing beautifully across the hall. The teacher remarked that she would never forget the feeling of encouragement Mignon gave her when

In our archives is an interesting letter written to Mignon Payne (her salary at this time was $185 a month):

> *December 18, 1958*
>
> *Dear Mrs. Payne:*
>
> *I am pleased to inform you that your salary has been raised $3.75 per month extra, retroactive to November 1st. The enclosed monthly check for December should show an additional $7.50 over last month's check.*
>
> *I am pleased that the Board of Trustees has been able to grant this additional fee, and hope it makes your Christmas more merry.*
>
> *Sincerely yours,*
> *Lawrence C. Lobaugh*
> *Headmaster*

she said, "The children sing better for you than they do for me." The teacher continued, "I'm not sure that was true, but Mignon really did boost my morale." According to her, Mignon used music to teach everything from mathematics to dancing.

Another teacher remembers the warm rapport Mrs. Payne created among those who worked for her. She allowed her teachers the freedom to be creative, and there was always an atmosphere of fun present in the school room.

She was insistent that children feel a sense of accomplishment, urging teachers to send small tokens of achievement home with them. Mignon initiated "The Thousand Club," for the children that were ready for a challenge.

To belong to this club, the student wrote on paper the number one and continued as far as the student could go. If he or she reached the goal of 1000, a roll of paper on which was written all the numbers, was sent home for the parents to see. She never pushed this; it was only for children who wanted more to do and to encourage them to accept a challenge.

Sydney Bates, who taught for many years in the Kindergarten, spoke of her high regard for Mignon in *The Tatler*:

> I will miss the joys of our friendship. There were many times when we lost patience with each other. There were times when we knew each other's thoughts. We shared many a story that only a Kindergarten teacher could appreciate. I will miss those jokes about her grasshopper pies, the antiquing jaunts to find glasses to match Grandfather Shenault's wine set, the late night phone conversations to hash out a school problem, Mignon's raised eyebrows and 'that look' when the chapel service presented its usual comic happenings, her calm acceptance of my ranting and raging over a nagging personal problem, her touching notes thanking me for some small kindness.

A former student expressed her love for Mrs. Payne in a memorial article also written for *The Tatler*:

> If the idea that learning was fun had not been implanted into my mind by Mrs. Payne, neither St. Mary's nor any other school would have been able to teach me what I now know. Mrs. Payne did not instill this love for learning and loving only in me, but in all the children that she came in contact with. Mrs. Payne made school a happy place for her children.

A Kindergarten library with books specifically for young children was given in memory of Mrs. Payne by teachers, former students, parents, and friends. There is also a beautiful piece of sculpture (pictured right) given by St. Mary's Mother's Club in her memory. The sculpture, created by Betsy Robbins, resides in the reception hall of Moss Hall and depicts a teacher receiving gifts from two small children. The library and this statue give credence to the high esteem and love in which she was held by those who worked with her and knew her.

In her article, she also mentioned that Mrs. Payne never forgot her former children. She often attended basketball and volleyball games, long after they had been in Kindergarten, cheering "her girls."

At the time of Mignon Payne's unexpected death, Mr. Leech wrote his thoughts about her to parents:

> We shall all miss Mrs. Payne. She was an outstanding primary educator whose influence in young lives was extremely good. Her counsel and common sense, exercised with rare grace, were memorable and appreciated by co-workers, by school trustees, by her many admirers. She will be sorely missed; in a certain sense she will not be replaced.

Helen Allen

Helen Allen came to St. Mary's in the fall of 1958 to teach social studies and history. Her students remember her tremendous knowledge of her subject matter and her enthusiasm in presenting it. They comment that "she instilled in her classes a love for history." According to one of her former students, Julia Alissandratos '63, her teaching of history "was animated by extracurricular interest and participation in state and local politics." She also mentioned that, "Mrs. Allen was the strength they often turned to during the long days of their trying adolescent years."

Although a strict disciplinarian, but always fair, her students had great respect and admiration for her. In the spring of 1962, she was appointed Principal of the Upper School, a position which she administered until her resignation in December 1963. Katharine Phillips who followed her as Acting Principal, complimented Mrs. Allen for "leaving everything in order; she had even written all the college recommendations for the seniors!"

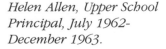

Helen Allen, Upper School Principal, July 1962-December 1963.

5. SCHOOL ATTAINS ACCREDITATION

First Headmaster — Lawrence C. Lobaugh

*Lawrence C. Lobaugh,
Headmaster 1958-1962.*

As I read Mr. Lobaugh's *Memoirs*, I realize they show his deep affection for St. Mary's and its students. After he resigned, he kept in close contact by correspondence and visited St. Mary's several times. I met him on one of his visits and was impressed by his gracious manner and his interest in all the developments of the school. One thing I have always been curious about is his reason for leaving a large public school in Long Island to become a Headmaster of a small independent school in the South. Perhaps it was due to George Phillips' persuasive manner.

By 1958, St. Mary's had grown so rapidly that it was in need of an experienced head to operate a high school. This was necessary to fulfill Gilmore Lynn's vision of St. Mary's again being a full twelve-year school. Under the leadership of George Phillips, Chairman, the Board of Trustees chose Mr. Lawrence C. Lobaugh to be St. Mary's first Headmaster. He had been superintendent of schools in Lindenhurst, New York, for eleven years, and was indeed knowledgeable about administration.

Fortunately, he left his *Memoirs* with the school. They reveal a flavor of his personality and life of the school under his leadership. His B.S. degree in ceramic engineering was from Alfred University. After graduation from college in 1927, he remarked that he was offered twice the salary he could make as a ceramic engineer to be a high school athletics coach. When talking about this, he laughingly said, "I'd probably be making twice as much today as a ceramic

Lobaugh's first day at St. Mary's was a surprising one. It began by his asking George Phillips "to show him his office." He was led into a storage room that had been cleaned for an office, but interestingly had no furniture. From his description, even after raiding the cellar to equip his office, the furniture consisted only of "two sad-looking chairs of uncertain strength and a dilapidated desk." The next question he asked was, "Do I have a secretary?" He quickly discovered there was no secretary. He was fortunate that Mrs. Jean Cone, one of the School's Trustees, volunteered to be Acting Secretary. "Without her," he remarked, "I would have been sunk."

engineer than I'm presently making in education." He graduated with a Master's degree in administration from New York University and continued his education at several universities including Illinois, Wisconsin, Syracuse and Hofstra College.

Mr. and Mrs. Lobaugh had three children—two daughters, Diane and Sally, and a son, Larry, who was tragically killed during his late teenage years in an automobile accident on Long Island. Each year at Class Day, there is an Lawrence Lobaugh Award given in their son's memory to a St. Mary's student athlete who exhibits good sportsmanship and who, above all, possesses the highest of personal qualities.

When the Board of Trustees presented Mr. Lobaugh the task of becoming St. Mary's first Headmaster, he requested that the Board give him full supervision and control of the school with a three- year contract. The Trustees' specific challenge to him included enlarging the school, improving its academic curriculum, and developing its physical facilities. Another requirement was to apply for and to receive accreditation from the State and from the Southern Association of Colleges and Secondary Schools. The school had no endowment; tuition had to take care of improvements to the school as well as current expenses. When he arrived in 1958, he discovered that school equipment was needed, registration was low, and classes had only a single section of each grade.

This new position was quite a change from his former one, where he had 500 teachers, 7500 students and five secretaries. St. Mary's consisted of approximately 20 teachers and 200 students. When he first accepted this position as Headmaster, Mr. Lobaugh realized it would be a challenge, but the extent of his challenge, as he began his tenure, was only beginning to become evident.

Changes and improvements had to be made. In order to improve St. Mary's academic standing, each applicant was required to take an admission test. A Teacher's Institute was also added. The purpose was to "cover the basic aims and ideals of the school, its philosophy, and methods of teaching." Mr. Lobaugh, as well as other teachers who had years of experience, led this Institute. This Institute existed during all his four years at the school, and met for several days before the opening of each school year. "The result," according to Mr. Lobaugh, "was that on the very first day of school, everything ran as smoothly as though it had been in session for days."

A 1959 Press/Scimitar *article stated that St. Mary's School was going to double its faculty:* St. Mary's Episcopal School will double its enrollment and faculty next fall, Headmaster L.C. Lobaugh said … 15 teachers have already been added in anticipation of an enrollment of more than 400 students. The school had 215 students and 15 teachers last term.

The Reverend Greenwood leads students in prayer.

By the fall of 1959, St. Mary's had almost doubled its enrollment to 400 students and increased its faculty to 30. The next task was to find more space for all the students who were eager to enroll. In 1960, George P. Phillips, St. Mary's Chairman of the Board, announced that construction would begin on a new church building which would provide classrooms for the school. This meant there would be space for additional classrooms with a particular emphasis on courses in scientific subjects and foreign languages. As mentioned earlier, this building was named Greenwood for the Reverend Eric Greenwood, at that time Rector of the Church of the Holy Communion.

Mr. Lobaugh's organizational ability soon became evident. As his tenure began, the only club available for the students was the Red Cross Club. A Student Council was formed, which began raising money by instigating paper drives and a Halloween Bazaar, an annual event and one of the school's main money raising activities. Memberships and charters were granted for the National Association of Student Councils, the National Honor Society, the National Beta Club, and the National Journalistic Society, Quill and Scroll. The dining room became a busy place. It provided space for school assemblies, visiting college representatives, annual spelling bees, and dramatic performances. Two choirs were formed, one for those with musical talent, the other for those who wanted to sing just for fun. In

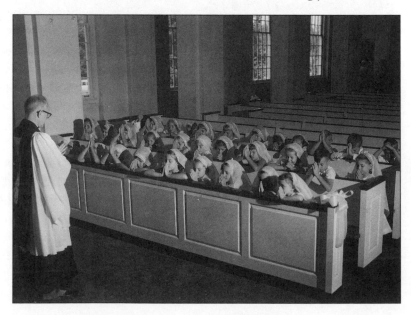

At the Halloween Bazaar.

1959 and 1960, St. Mary's published its first annual with Beverly Burkett '61 as editor-in-chief. It was appropriately named the *Carillon* for the bells in the church. A school newspaper entitled *The Chimes* was published in 1960-61, which later became *The Tatler*, a name used in the early 1900s. Other extra-curricular activities were insti-gated such as annual school plays, freshmen initiation, and Class Day.

One of the important items on his agenda was to set in motion steps for St. Mary's to be accredited by the State Education Association. It took two years for this to be accomplished, but then St. Mary's successfully made the Certified List and was accredited by the State of Tennessee in 1960. In the fall of 1961, after three years of work, application was made for accreditation by the Southern Association of Colleges and Secondary Schools. The Examining Committee of this Association spent three days investigating all facets of the school, but no definitive answer was given to the school until the fall of 1962, at which time it was accredited. By the end of Mr. Lobaugh's four years at St. Mary's, the school was accepted as a member of the following: the National Education Association, the National Association of Secondary School Principals, the National Association of Private Schools, the American Association of School Administrators, and the Memphis Independent School Association.

Mr. Lobaugh felt a new design was needed for the school's offi-cial logo; this was designed by a Memphis jeweler. The logo

The original design of St. Mary's seal designed in 1958 by senior Katharine Phillips '61.

The symbol for the Belles of St. Mary's.

consisted of Greek letters placed in the inner circle of a round design, meaning Light and Life, and St. Mary's Episcopal School appeared in the outer circle. It was used on stationery, official documents, and jewelry. Many items such as notebooks, pennants, dolls, pillows, and T-shirts with the St. Mary's logo were sold in the school bookstore which he established the first year.

His next decision was to design a symbol for the school. When Mr. Lobaugh first arrived in Memphis, he nicknamed the St. Mary's girls, "The Belles." Accordingly, he felt a suitable symbol "would be a Southern girl, dressed in a hoop skirt with a bonnet headpiece, and holding in her hands a metal hoop that was popular to roll in bygone days." Evidently, the model he had in mind was an eighteenth century "Southern Belle" and this symbol was used on programs and advertising. This symbol is definitely not a picture of the St. Mary's girl of today or actually of the past 30 years. It was, however, used as a symbol for many years, but officially dropped in the '70s to be replaced by the Turkey, which continues to be St. Mary's mascot.

The Mother's Club came into existence during his tenure and performed many needed functions, such as purchasing necessary equipment for the school—visual aids, movie and slide projectors, and maps. During American Education Week, the school had its first Parents' Night for the purpose of informing the parents about the aims and objectives of the school, for them to see their child's classroom, and for them to become acquainted with her teacher and the Headmaster. In the spring, there was another Parents' Night for the parents to observe the Upper School science exhibits and art work.

An academic, four-year program was developed for the Upper School to prepare students for admission to colleges and universities. An up-to-date science room was added for the purpose of teaching general science, biology, chemistry, and physics (taught in alternate years). College Board Tests and the American College Testing Programs were instituted for the Upper School as well as the National Merit Scholarship Program for juniors.

Mr. Lobaugh's *Memoirs* compliment Mrs. Lynn and Mrs. Parker on their leadership of the school. He believed they were the cement that held St. Mary's together through very trying years. They managed to keep alive several traditions, such as the Christmas Pageant and May Day, the latter under the leadership of Mrs. Derek Rooke. He emphasized strongly that there was a wonderful St. Mary's spirit

Mother's Club Board: (seated, left to right) Mrs. Don Gordon, Mrs. Margaret Stepherson, Mrs. Ben Carrick, and Mrs. Richard Maury; (standing) Mrs. Dixon Jordon, Mrs. H.H. Work, Mrs. Cooper Adams, Mrs. W.W. Watkins, Mrs. Fred Boehme, Mrs. E.H. Tenent, Mrs. L.H. Haglund, Mrs. Forrest Ladd, and Mrs. Winston Hoover.

that pervaded the School. It was found in chapel services, in classrooms, in every cooperative effort, and more importantly was lived from day-to-day by both the students and the faculty.

In return, the faculty recognized and respected his organizational ability, but there was one facet each teacher recalls vividly and with some humor. He put a time clock in his receptionist's office, that each teacher was asked to use. He also was a copious master of writing notes to the teachers, filled, they thought, with minutiae. They knew the school was managed more efficiently, but it was run similarly to a large public school rather than to a small independent one. Nonetheless, he was an efficient administrator, and he successfully answered St. Mary's needs for that particular time.

Mr. Lobaugh left St. Mary's in 1962 "with sadness" to accept a position as Professor of Education and Assistant Director of Admissions at C.W. Post College of Long Island University. During the years following his resignation from St. Mary's, he demonstrated his attachment and love for the students by sending a graduation gift to each member of the classes he had known during his years as

Class of 1961, the first class to graduate since 1949, pictured at the Holy Communion Church.

Headmaster. In his *Memoirs*, he reminds us of this feeling about the school: "I enjoyed my four years in Memphis, and I believe I left part of my heart there, because my love and faith in this fine school has continued throughout my thirteen years away from it." His dedication to the spiritual life is also revealed in his *Memoirs* which conclude with the following advice to seniors:

> Each human being bears the name and mark of the Master Architect. We are made by His hand. Each of us is of infinite value, never to be discarded as worthless. God has put the stamp of supreme value upon each of us. We are His. Every person may claim his or her place as a child of God … You will find your place in the sun.

In his four years at St. Mary's, Mr. Lobaugh fulfilled the challenge given to him by the Board of Trustees. The school received accreditation and grew in size. Its physical facilities were developed, and its academic curriculum was improved. He is remembered gratefully for successfully laying the groundwork for those who followed him.

6. DEVELOPING ITS OWN IDENTITY

Nathaniel Cheairs Hughes, Jr.
Headmaster 1962-1973

N at Hughes was St. Mary's Headmaster and my superior, but primarily, I will always think of him as my teacher. I depended on his strength as an educator and administrator and was the fortunate recipient of his wise advice and counsel. These were great years to be associated with St. Mary's; they were a time of growth and expansion. The school was inspired by its former leaders and by a Headmaster who

Nathaniel Cheairs Hughes, Jr.,
Ph.D., Headmaster 1962-1973.

When offering the position to Dr. Nathaniel Cheairs Hughes Jr., Mr. Phillips surprised him by asking the question: "How would you like to come to Memphis and run a girls' school?" This was an appropriate question as Dr. Hughes had been in an all boys' school and had, at that time, two sons of his own. After visiting Memphis and St. Mary's, Dr. Hughes remarked, "I saw an opportunity and need there and agreed to take the job." His career as Headmaster began in July 1962.

wanted to make their dreams come true. As I write about him, I realize the impact of his years at St. Mary's and the debt the school owes him for emphasizing the academic and spiritual legacy of the school.

Once again, George Phillips was instrumental in selecting a Headmaster. He seemed to have the knack for finding the best person for a particular time. His choice was exactly right.

Nat Hughes graduated from Messick High School in Memphis, and completed his undergraduate work at Yale University. Following his graduation from college, he was in the Marine Corps from 1953-55, and, as he phrased it, "gained the confidence necessary to pursue a teaching career," which was exactly what he wanted. He earned his M.A. and Ph.D. degrees in history from the University of North Carolina, where he served as teaching fellow and departmental assistant from 1955-1959. His dissertation, later published as a novel, was entitled *General William J. Hardee, C.S.A.* Since that time, he has written many books about the Civil War, short stories, articles, and book reviews.

Dr. Hughes taught at Webb School from 1959-1962 as teacher of three levels of history and eighth grade Latin; he was a college counselor, chairman of the discipline committee, dorm supervisor, person in charge of one-fourth of student body, and football coach. This list of his responsibilities at Webb made me understand why he expected so much of his faculty.

Dr. Hughes married Buckner Latimore from Chattanooga, a graduate of Vassar College, whom he met while he was at Yale. They have three sons, Frank, David, and Sam, who was born after they came to Memphis. It did not take long for St. Mary's to appreciate both Nat and Bucky Hughes. An article in the *Press/Scimitar* stated that, "from all indications it's a case of 'love at first sight' between parents, pupils and trustees of St. Mary's Episcopal School and their new Headmaster and his wife, Bucky."

Teaching was his heritage. He had never known his grandfather, William Hughes, co-founder of Branham and Hughes Academy in Spring Hill, Tennessee, but "he was very much alive in our family" and was one of the reasons Hughes decided on education as a career. His grandfather was encouraged to enter the educational field by W.R. "Sawny" Webb of Webb School, where Nat Hughes later taught for three years. Dr. Hughes was an admirer of both these

> *I am here to guide— teachers are the ones to make it happen.*
> —*Dr. Nathaniel Hughes, Jr.*

men, and his career as Headmaster was influenced by their lives and their philosophy of education.

Dr. Hughes welcomed the challenge St. Mary's offered him with great interest and enthusiasm which spilled over very quickly to the faculty, and student body. He was young, personable, a dedicated historian, and a teacher who wanted to be a Headmaster. As he began his first year at St. Mary's, a new wave of optimism seized the Board of Trustees and the entire St. Mary's family. It took only a short time for him to recognize the potential for greatness that existed at St. Mary's, but he also realized the school would have to change to meet his expectations and vision. His dream, as he described it to the faculty, board, and parents, was for St. Mary's to be the best academic school in Memphis, in Tennessee, in the South, and in fact anywhere. He described himself "as a one-man war against mediocrity." He admitted freely that St. Mary's should be a "tough" school and that any education worthy of being called an education was not a comfortable process. Several alumnae remember Dr. Hughes saying, "Students are not being educated here to decorate a golf course." He believed whole-heartedly that St. Mary's could be a great school, and, as a consequence, others became believers and followers of his vision.

Academic excellence was a must with Dr. Hughes; he demanded the best of his teachers. Added to that, he made everyone feel indispensable. According to one teacher, even though a person was not certified, he was willing to give applicants who wanted to teach an opportunity to do so. Then he would counsel and encourage them to complete the required work for certification. Long before the person involved realized it, he seemed to see the promise in an individual. This I know, for his belief in me was a constant challenge to persevere through some difficult moments.

Dr. Hughes encouraged fun and laughter. Teachers often remarked, "It was fun to teach at St. Mary's." A former student and faculty member, Jeanne Stevenson Moessner '66, emphasizes strongly that a sense of humor pervaded the school, and she believes that this attitude is one of the reasons why St. Mary's has existed over such a long period of time.

Slowly, Hughes' dream for St. Mary's developed. He worked long hours a day, inspiring others to give wholeheartedly in their own special fields of endeavor. His attitude and concern for his staff

A cartoon that appeared in The Tatler *reveals Dr. Hughes' philosophy—school is always open despite even the most difficult weather conditions.*

The following appeared in the November, 1965 issue of The Tennessee Churchman:

Memphis Day School Tops the State Merit Semi-Finalists

A secondary objective of St. Mary's is academic excellence and it has been suggested that this objective be discussed more fully. In 1965, St. Mary's had five Merit Semi-Finalists out of a senior class of seventeen, which is the highest per-centage of any prepara-tory school, private or public, in the state of Tennessee. This fact may mean several things, but we at St. Mary's regard it as meaning that a girl with good normal ability who applies herself can succeed beyond what usually has been expected.

and faculty made it all seem worthwhile. As one secretary said, "He makes me feel special." It is no wonder St. Mary's matured so rapidly during his tenure.

It was through Dr. Hughes' vision and determination that St. Mary's rebuilt its reputation as an outstanding college preparatory school, not only in Memphis, but also in the South and throughout the country. It became a school known for excellence in whatever it undertook. Part of this reputation was the result of the high per-centage of Merit Scholars at St. Mary's. In 1966, there were five National Merit Scholars in a class of only 17 students. Ever since that year, the school has had an enviable record in the National Merit Scholarship Program as a result of its excellent academic curriculum.

Dr. Hughes' love of teaching led him to teach a Great Books class to seniors. The students who took the course had to write sev-eral papers each year. One alumna remembers he had a big red stamp with the word "bull" written on it in 2 1/2 to 3 inch letters. Ever since, she has judged her writing by the criteria of Dr. Hughes' "red bull." She became her own self-critic, and says, "I shall always be indebted to Nat Hughes for that 'red bull.'"

Nat had a special style all his own. Most often he is remembered as wearing a beige sweater with leather patches and Hush Puppy shoes, and continuously striking matches to light his pipe. He thor-oughly enjoyed communicating with students and faculty on an informal basis. Each morning he arrived early, to go to a room off the cafeteria (actually a smoking room for Nat and his teachers) to communicate with the "early-bird" faculty members. There was a great deal of teasing and laughing in that room. These moments cre-ated a special beginning to the day and are remembered fondly by his faculty. One teacher remembers that he

> often talked admiringly about one teacher to another, but always in her presence so that she could hear the compli-ments ... His counsel and advice, always wise, were so deftly delivered that the receiver generally thought that she had not only discovered the problem but solved it herself.

During his early years as Headmaster, Dr. Hughes instituted a training session for the Board of Trustees, emphasized and increased the endowment fund created by George Phillips in the 1950s with $1,000 and encouraged teachers to attend educational workshops. He also appointed a director of the Alumnae Association to organize

Alumnae Day, 1965: (seated) Mary Love '04, and Octavia Love '07; (standing) Patti Person, Joyce Burkett, and Cathy Hoover (class of '65).

the yearly celebration of Alumnae Day. These observances helped tie the St. Mary's of the 1960s to the St. Mary's alumnae who had attended the school from the 1920s to the 1940s.

One of Dr. Hughes' ambitions was to have a closer connection between St. Mary's Cathedral and St. Mary's School. The gift of an 85-year-old carriage stone from St. Mary's Cathedral to the school emphasized this relationship. This historic moment took place in the spring of 1964. The stone was moved from the Cathedral to the grounds of the school at Perkins Extended and Walnut Grove Road with the proviso that it would always remain at the school. During the early years of the school, when it had been at the Cathedral, the students had used this stone to enter a carriage. In 1964, a special ceremony was arranged, complete with horse and carriage. Those

Formal presentation of carriage stone to St. Mary's School on Perkins Extended by St. Mary's Cathedral: (left to right) Dr. Hughes, Ada Raines '10, Marion West '65, Russell Perry, Bishop's Warden, and Grover Secord, owner of the carriage.

riding in the carriage were Miss Ada Raines, '07, an alumna, Marion West '65, a student, Russell Perry, Bishop's Warden at the school, and Grover Secord, owner of the carriage in which they rode to the ceremony. Another occasion that cemented the relationship between the Cathedral and St. Mary's was a visitation to the Cathedral one Sunday each spring by the student body, outfitted in their cottas. For years, they rode buses from the Sears Roebuck parking lot to the Cathedral where they walked down the aisle and participated in the service.

When the elementary school moved to Moss Hall, chapel was still held in the church for the Middle and Upper Schools daily, but the Lower School now has its own chapel in Starnes Common.

> Dr. Hughes continued the requirement that all students, grades one through twelve, be present at chapel every morning. Shelley Fraser, an elementary teacher for many years remembered:
>
> > Each day we walked into chapel with our white starched chapel caps, and thought, 'This is the day the Lord has made.' Love was there in the chapel and in the school. When we sang 'The Saints of God,' it made us all wish we could be saints too.

During the early sixties, there were many new developments at St. Mary's. The installation of a scholarship program was partially endowed in 1963 and a goal established to have a least 20% of the student body receive financial aid. One of the first scholarships established was the endowed Hazlehurst Memorial Scholarship, given in 1965 by Jean Hazlehurst Cone in memory of her mother, Charlotte Stemmler Hazlehurst '05. Both teachers' retirement and enrichment programs also began.

One of the most important accomplishments during Dr. Hughes' tenure was the establishment of the St. Mary's School's Honor Council. Although honor had always been emphasized strongly at St. Mary's, the Honor Council was introduced officially to St. Mary's in 1962, modeled on the one at Webb School in Bell Buckle, Tennessee. Honor as a way of life continues to be of supreme importance in the life of the school.

In 1964, *The Tatler* published its first edition since the twenties. The editor was Carol Sue Cato '64 and the advisor, Miss Peggy O'Sullivan, former English teacher. A column entitled, "Ann Slanders," mentioned a subject that might have been written in the 1990s.

> I was thoroughly disgusted with your last article that said that St. Mary's students should only have to study 10 hours a night. This is ridiculous. In view of the fact that we are at home 16 hours a day on week days, we should all study 15 and 36/97 of these hours, leaving the remaining time for sleeping, bathing or any other such minor diversions.
>
> — Thoroughly Disgusted

Some things never change! Other articles in this issue, similar to *The Tatler* of today, are about athletic events and current activities such as "St. Mary's Varsity Basketball Team Defeats St. Agnes," "Students Enter Writing Contest," and "Dramatists Begin Play Rehearsals." *The Tatler* has continued to be an important part of the school's life and is a highly treasured tradition.

Also, in the mid-1960s, another literary magazine, *Belles Lettres*, came into existence. In the introduction, the editor, Ellen Rumsey, wrote, "These pages represent only a small part of the excellent writing that is done in our school everyday." The staff included the following: Susan Dacus '66, Mary Lawrence Hughes '66, Claire McCaskill '66, Kathy Roop '66, Jane Allen '67, Elinor Baker '68, Caroline Cloninger '68, Nora Heflin '69, Marta Richards '69, and Mary Helene Lee '68. This is published annually.

Several money-raising projects were initiated by the students in the sixties. One was the weekly bake sale. The first year these sales made the unbelievable amount of $895.64 from the cooking efforts of the students and their mothers. This money was used to purchase curtains for the gymnasium. Another very popular and successful money-raising activity was the Halloween Bazaar, initiated and run by the Student Council.

Also in the mid-1960s, St. Mary's Board of Trustees declined an opportunity to "pursue conversations with Lausanne School about combining the two Upper Schools on the Lausanne Campus in East Memphis." Instead, St. Mary's began its first building fund in 1967. The school was in desperate need of administrative offices, classrooms, an assembly hall, a library, science labs, and art studios. Under the chairmanship of E. W. "Ned" Cook, its goal was to raise $400,000. Enrollment had increased to 562 girls in a space designed originally for 250, according to John T. Fisher, Chairman of the Board of Trustees and campaign vice-chairman. Ned Cook remarked that these new facilities would insure "continued high-caliber education" for the girls at St. Mary's. He added, "The caliber of work produced is in direct proportion to the tools available. Without extravagance, the new building will offer these tools." Dr. Hughes had similar thoughts:

> This building will allow St. Mary's to give greater emphasis to the areas of science and fine arts. The library will promote independent study and an atmosphere in keeping with a serious academic tradition … Other features in the building will help centralize the elementary school and the high school and give badly needed flexibility to both. The building would go far toward disentangling St. Mary's from the day by day operation of the Church of the Holy Communion, thus avoiding interfering with the church's progress. The Library, and Fine Arts Building, specifically designed for educational purposes, would fill the acute need for adequate facilities and would enable St. Mary's to carry out her aims and goals.

The new building on Perkins Extended was completed in 1968 and named for a former St. Mary's student and generous donor to the building fund, Mrs. Elizabeth Brinkley Taylor. Her grandson, James B. Taylor, Jr., presently serves as Chairman of St. Mary's Board of Trustees, and she is the great-grandmother of two St. Mary's students,

Courtney and Lawrence Taylor. Dr. Hughes emphasized that the construction of the Taylor Building provided the necessary facilities for an ambitious high school program and strengthened the concept of an independent school. With this decision, St. Mary's had its own street address distinct from the Church of the Holy Communion and employed its own maintenance staff.

In a report to the vestry, Dr. Hughes described the school in two ways:

> *Quantitatively*: St. Mary's has an enrollment of 500 students with forty faculty members ... St. Mary's derives 96% of its operating funds from tuition and about 4% from gifts from our student organizations and our 1000 alumnae ...

> *Qualitatively*: Our methods and objectives have been tested over a period of ninety-one years and have been found to be successful. In professional academic circles in the Mid-South, this school is highly regarded. For example, Vincent de Frank, (former conductor of Memphis Symphony Orchestra) says 'our music program is the most advanced in the Memphis area.' Among the school children of Memphis, St. Mary's is known as a tough school, with lots of spirit which will compete against you in any activity at any place and at any time ... Although St. Mary's is not a school for egg-heads, it most definitely is not a school for the unintelligent, the undisciplined, the unmotivated. It is designed to provide for parents who want their children to have a stimulating intellectual program in a Christian environment.

St. Mary's has the distinction of being the first independent school in Memphis to integrate its student body. This was in 1968 and was a traumatic and serious decision by the Board of Trustees and Dr. Hughes. Because of public school integration, many parents were enrolling their children in all-white private schools. When St. Mary's decided to integrate, some of the parents were concerned, and one class lost almost half of its students. That year was a difficult time, but it proved to be moment of truth. The decision to integrate demonstrated the school's convictions and proved its courage by upholding them. One of the results was that St. Mary's character was recognized by the community and the school became known not only for its academic excellence, but also for its moral strength. Anne Fisher, art teacher, remembers a teacher in a faculty meeting before the opening of school that year asking, "How we could prepare the students for the arrival of two black students ... entering as seventh

The Board of Trustees of St. Mary's Episcopal School
requests the honor of your presence
at
the Centennial Celebration of the Founding of the School
and
the Dedication of the New Building
on All Saints' Day
Friday, the first of November
at two o'clock in the afternoon
60 Perkins Extended

Invitation to the Centennial Celebration, November 1, 1968.

E.W. "Ned" Cook, Chairman of the campaign for the new building, speaking at the Centennial Celebration.

graders?" Nat's reply was "You have already prepared them. St. Mary's students know what's right, and they will know how to behave." He was right; they did.

It is heart-warming to know these minority students, first admitted in 1968 and warmly accepted by the student body, continued at St. Mary's, graduating with the class of 1974.

The hundredth anniversary of the founding of the school was planned originally for 1969, for it had been assumed for many years that 1869 was the original founding date. Despite research by Dr. Hughes' history students who discovered an earlier date, the decision was made to go ahead with the plans for the celebration in 1969. It proved to be a remarkable occasion. The entire Upper School, along with the faculty and Board of Trustees, robed in their caps and

Presentation during the Centennial Celebration of Dr. Hughes' portrait to the school, painted by Marshall Bouldin, a gift from the class of 1968. On the stairway: Dr. Hughes, Newton Allen, Chairman of the Board of Trustees, Deborah Pigott '68, Class President, and John T. Fisher, Trustee.

gowns, processed to the front of the new Taylor Building, which was being dedicated that same day. Dr. Thomas Corwin Mendenhall, president of Smith College, delivered the address; the Right Reverend John Vander Horst, Bishop of the Episcopal Diocese of Tennessee, gave the dedication address. Other dignitaries attending the service were Lawrence Lobaugh, former Headmaster, and Sister Christabel of St. Mary's on the Mountain at Sewanee, representing the Order of St. Mary. It was a beautiful day and a joyous occasion, even though the date of the founding of the school was not accurate. Following the service, a portrait of Dr. Hughes in full academic regalia, painted by Marshall Bouldin and given by the class of 1968, was unveiled in the library.

Dr. Hughes with students from the class of 1970: (left to right) Miki Scruggs, Susan Cooley, Kathy Baker, and Lynn Schadt.

During the early 1970s, another design was created for the school logo. This logo still contains the Greek letters meaning light and life and was designed by Tallie Moore Bush, a friend of Cynthia Pitcock, a former St. Mary's teacher. A beautiful banner, with this logo needlepointed on it by one of our librarians, Susie Goza, is used for the Lower School chapel.

In the program for the Centennial Celebration, Dr. Hughes wrote about "remembering," and reminded us of our heritage. He talked about Mary Pope, about Bishop Quintard, about the Sisters, about Miss Loomis and Miss Neely, about Mrs. Lynn, and about Lawrence Lobaugh, who was succeeded by Nat C. Hughes in 1962. He also stressed "the effort and love of students, alumnae, parents and behind them all, the support of the Episcopal Church." In his conclusion, he reminded us: "Our past sustains us; our past represents an ideal toward which we will always strive. We remember and we give thanks to God."

In 1972, Dr. Hughes reported to the November 27th Board meeting that Ellen Davies-Rodgers, who had done a great deal of research on the founding of Calvary Church, had determined that 1847 was the founding date of St. Mary's School. Mr. Newton Allen moved that the Board officially recognize 1847 as the founding date of St. Mary's Episcopal School; Mr. John Cawthon seconded the motion, and it passed unanimously.

Everyone connected with the school, myself included, knew Dr. Hughes was pugnacious in his attitude that St. Mary's must be the best in anything it undertook. This was particularly noticeable in his feeling about sports, for he was a competitor and never liked to lose. He challenged Presbyterian Day School's Kindergarten to a T-Ball

Basketball team with Dr. Hughes, their coach and most enthusiastic supporter.

game which St. Mary's won overwhelmingly. This was during the days when St. Mary's was co- ed (Kindergarten through third grade, 1953-1956). One player on St. Mary's team hit the ball and everyone shouted, "Johnny, run home!" Johnny did—and ran straight across the field towards his home on Perkins Street, directly in back of the school!

Dr. Hughes was concerned that St. Mary's did not have more competitive athletic teams, and decided, along with various teachers, to coach the varsity and seventh grade teams himself, a role which he enjoyed and worked at zealously. His secretary told a story which demonstrated his serious desire to win. She purchased two flags, one green and one red. The day after a game, if there was a red flag on her desk, it implied that this was not a day to make a request or even to visit him. On the other hand, if there was a green flag on the desk, it meant a successful game; the staff and faculty could brave his den without fear.

In his *Reflections*, written for this book about his years at St. Mary's, Dr. Hughes feels one of his most important decisions was that the school would become an independent Episcopal School. For this purpose, a charter of incorporation was obtained from the State of Tennessee, the Bishop of Tennessee joined the governing board as an ex-officio member, and the Rector of Calvary Church was elected as a regular member. Also, the old ties with St. Mary's Cathedral, Calvary Church, and St. Mary's School at Sewanee were re-established. The Catherine Neely Scholarship was established, and all the parishes of Shelby County were invited to nominate daughters of parishioners for this honor, signifying St. Mary's commitment to the Episcopal community of Shelby County and West Tennessee.

The school, already approved by the state, sought new academic direction by joining the Mid-South Association of Independent Schools and securing accreditation from the Southern Association of Schools and Colleges. "It thus regained freedom to develop the rich, flexible educational program that had characterized the school in the past when it had been a proprietary enterprise."

Dr. Hughes believes re-connection to the past and experimentation characterized his eleven years at St. Mary's. Many things were tried and failed: Greek as a foreign language, intramural sports, the

Liz Lansing (left) and Margaret Fayssoux (right), Administrative Secretaries par excellence.

Amazingly, Dr. Hughes' school office was run with … only three people, Doris Bard as Business Manager and Liz Lansing as Secretary/Office Manager/Director of Admissions, along with Virginia Gordon, secretary. Despite the lack of a large support staff, Nat never seemed too busy to stop and chat — and many days he sorted the incoming mail and put it in the faculty boxes himself.

chess club, an indoor May Day, Saturday School, and debate. Although enormous effort was given to the concept of the teacher-counselor relationship, it had disappointing results. As he mentioned, "These proved just side-steps, however, for the school that would lead the United States in the percentage of National Merit Semi-Finalists in 1966 and win wide acclaim for its superb Kindergarten program."

Dr. Hughes closed his recollections with the following statement:

> The heroes of this period when St. Mary's began to win recognition for its scholarship and its unusual ability to impact a girl positively were Gilmore Lynn, Katharine Phillips, Mignon Payne, and Mary Davis, not to speak of the school's brave and bold board of trustees and its noble faculty. Under their leadership and by their example the halls of St. Mary's echoed—'We can do it. It's our mission. Let's try.'

Dr. Hughes lived this statement during his years as Headmaster and inspired the faculty and students as well as the board with his positive and challenging approach to the education of girls. St. Mary's came alive during his tenure. At his resignation, *The Commercial Appeal* quoted Dr. Hughes' thoughts:

> The time has come for new leadership at St. Mary's. I have been the one to receive the education these past eleven years at St. Mary's Episcopal School; I've learned an appreciation of the special value of education of women and their leadership role in the community and society. I am utterly converted to that position—that education for women is one of the greatest needs in America. St. Mary's has completely sold me on that cause.

His bold vision for St. Mary's left a legacy that is still apparent. He managed to make the impossible possible.

Mary Davis

One of the surprises of living to age 87 is the discovery that life is still filled with many enjoyable opportunities. At least, I felt this way until I suddenly realized this book would not be an accurate story unless it included some of my personal memories. This made me wonder why this fact had not struck me before starting such an adventure. That is exactly what it has been—an exciting glimpse into

Mary McClintock Davis, Upper School Dean, 1964-73; Acting Headmistress, 1973-74 and spring semester, 1981.

the lives of the people who have dedicated themselves to this school. Until now, writing this book has been a thrilling experience, but to talk about my own activities and thoughts during my years here is soul-searching because they are the story of my own life for the past 33 years.

July 1, 1964, was my first day at St. Mary's; it was a memorable one. My office was actually a large closet. In a way, that was an advantage, for it made me feel close to the individuals who came to talk with me. I had two student callers; I am confident their purpose was to look me over. The first one, Suzanne Brescia '67, was seriously thinking of transferring to another school, and I didn't want

St. Mary's was filled with a small but enthusiastic group of teachers who believed in the philosophy of the school and in each other. They were there because they loved to teach and were infused with the dreams of the Headmaster. From the very first day, I felt welcomed. The whole year was truly a learning experience; the teachers, along with Katharine Phillips, Gilmore Lynn, and Nat Hughes, taught me in innumerable ways and never seemed tired of steering me in the right direction.

Class of 1965. First row (left to right): Susan Taylor, Patti Person, Marion West, Joyce Burkett. Second row: Julia Malone, Lucy Minor, Sally Pace, Kathy Sweany, Liz Pryor, Janet Peters, Susan Hoefer, Janice Donelson, Kathy Hoover and Ellen Rumsey. (Not pictured: Mimi Eisenbeis.)

to be the one to send her there. By some good fortune, we started talking about sports, a mutual interest, and from then on, the conversation flowed easily. My next caller, Julia Malone '65, was the president of the Student Council. I was almost intimidated by her confidence and intelligence. Fortunately, for the school and for me, she was an excellent leader—full of energy and creative ideas. I particularly liked her forthrightness and sincerity. She introduced me to student activities at St. Mary's and gave me insight into my relationships with the girls.

In 1964, there were 154 students in the Upper School (grades 7-12) so we became acquainted very quickly. Amazingly, we all lived on the third floor of Greenwood Building. It was a cozy place, especially when someone tried to open a locker, for then no one could move in the halls. Nightmares were a frequent companion of mine, for I feared the disastrous result of a fire. Much to the dismay of the faculty, we did have frequent fire drills and learned to empty the building in one minute, demonstrating the speed with which we could move, if necessary.

Chapel was, as it still is, a very special part of the day for all of us. We are especially indebted to the Rectors of the Church of the Holy Communion for their cooperation and support. I remember the Reverend Eric Greenwood's love of music and his teaching the great

The Reverend Daniel Matthews, Assistant Priest, Church of the Holy Communion, receives a gold cross from the school, presented by Jeanne Stevenson '66.

St. Mary's Alma Mater:

St. Mary's, St. Mary's, shine thy guiding light
Down every dark pathway, and lead us aright.
Let thy truth eternal illumine our way
And grant us thy wisdom to guide us each day.

—*Lauren McMahon '69*

hymns of the church; the Reverend Dan Matthews' spiritual homilies appealing to everyone from the youngest first grader to the oldest faculty member; the Reverend Harold Barrett's preaching erudite sermons; the Reverend Reynolds Cheney's showing warmth and love through some very difficult moments. Every student from first through twelfth grade was required to be present for chapel and one of the joys of leading the service during the second semester was hearing first graders, who had just become readers, read the psalm very slowly. They would continue, never stopping, even after everyone else had finished. As they were completing the psalm, their little voices, heard by those around them, surrounded us with a feeling of community and of love. We left chapel with our spirits lifted.

Cheerleaders show their spirit.

Athletics became a very important part of the school. In the 1960s and '70s, we belonged to a league called MIGS, Memphis Independent Girls' Schools. This league consisted of five independent schools: St. Agnes, Miss Hutchison's, Immaculate Conception, Lausanne, and St. Mary's. MIGS had its own organization with a co-ordinator, Janet Sheehan, who arranged the schedule and hired the referees. The rivalry was particularly intense between St. Mary's, St. Agnes, and Hutchison. It was a much less complicated organization than the present one, but there was a great deal of enthusiasm. We even had cheerleaders wearing their colorful uniforms. It was *the* place to be on Tuesdays and Thursdays after school, and the gyms were crowded; students, faculty, and parents attended. One decided advantage was that the games were played in the afternoons and the girls could be home before six. For several years, I remember the Mother's Club organized a Mother/Daughter basketball game which created excitement, and one year we had a Father/Daughter volleyball game. These competitive games were all wonderful spirit builders.

Memories keep flooding back as I think about that first year. I especially remember with joy and surprise my first Christmas Pageant, beautiful beyond description, and my first commencement, with the seniors in their white dresses accompanied by shy but captivating flower girls. I am reminded of my first talk on "behavior" to the students in chapel when I wondered if anyone was really listening, and then, much to my surprise, they walked out of the chapel in total silence.

I found there were many concerned and caring girls who had a desire to reach out beyond the school; a group went to Hanley, a public school in Orange Mound, every week to tutor, giving up their study hall and lunch hour. I also discovered every student needed individual attention and that each one had something special about her.

Moving to the newly constructed Taylor Building in 1969 was an exciting time. Our main movers were the students themselves and some of their brothers and friends. With many groans and much laughter, they moved the entire library from the third floor of Greenwood to the main library on the first floor of Taylor. This library under the supervision of Helen Fentress didn't contain many books or even shelves for them, but Helen was filled with ideas for acquiring them, which, little by little, she accomplished. The library was carpeted and had a balcony, and in our estimation, was the perfect place to study and to read.

I was thrilled with my new office, for it was ideally located on the second floor, near most of the Upper School classes. Through my window, I had a view of the church steeple, a constant source of relaxation and inspiration. My secretaries were terrific. My morning secretary was Margaret Fayssoux, whose specialty was typing all the transcripts perfectly, and my afternoon secretary, Carolyn Heppel, kept me organized and on schedule.

Mary Davis and Nat Hughes in front of her new office.

Dr. Hughes' resignation in 1973 was a sad moment for all of us. To my consternation and surprise, I was asked to be Acting Headmistress for the 1973-74 year. I agonized over it all summer,

We worked hard and managed to have a lot of fun, but also suffered some tense moments. Occasionally, we misplaced files, lost papers, and once in a while, students. We found them in some interesting places, like the church's restroom (out-of- bounds, of course) and on the roof of the library. One day, our nerves were almost shattered by three of our students being so agitated over a burglar robbing their "senior den," that they chased him all the way to the Union Planters Bank on Poplar where they caught him. The news of this "triumph" was even reported in the next day's The Commercial Appeal.

and then suddenly I realized that I had little cause to worry. I had a wonderful faculty and staff: a dedicated Acting Dean, Mary Hills (Presh) Gill, a most supportive Chairman of the Board of Trustees, Tom Johnston, an excellent Business Manager, Doris Bard, and the one and only Liz Lansing as secretary. They would be doing the work. From that moment on, I knew it would be all right. I remember it as a good year; the faculty and staff remember it as the "only year they received a Christmas bonus!"

The Sisters initiated the custom of faculty and students wearing chapel caps daily to chapel. This continued to 1973. At the beginning of each year, the homeroom mother would wash and iron these caps, sending them to school in a crisp, clean condition. This lasted no longer than a week or two, and then the caps began turning gray, even black, and were quickly torn and ragged. Nevertheless, they had to be worn.

In the fall of 1973, I decided to do away with the requirement of wearing chapel caps. It was a difficult decision for me, because it was the breaking of a long tradition. Speaking personally, although a Presbyterian, the wearing of these caps was, in a way, an outward expression of an inward feeling, just as kneeling to pray is another form of worship. It made me feel, "This is a special moment." It was, however, a great relief for the mothers and for the teachers who were responsible for keeping these chapel caps in order and on the students' heads.

I was glad to welcome Reverend David Leech as Headmaster in July 1974, and to turn over the responsibility of being head of the school. Our years of working together were very pleasant ones for me. In 1979, I suddenly woke up to the thought that I had passed the conventional retirement age, and I knew the time was drawing near for me to retire as Dean, which I did in December 1979. The Board of Trustees, the faculty, and the parents gave an unbelievable retirement party for me and, of all surprising things, a trip to China, where I was born. It was an unforgettable evening, especially watching the faculty wind down the stairs singing "A Slow Boat to China" to present me with a miniature boat made by Barbara Mansberg, Spanish teacher, and her husband, Roy. My entire family was there—a total surprise. Love and thoughtfulness were apparent throughout the entire evening. To be the recipient of such kindness was overwhelming.

The transition from Dean to another position was a difficult one for me, for I missed my close association with the Upper School faculty and students. Each one was a special friend, and for a time, I felt lost without their daily companionship. Although my years as Dean were extremely busy and filled with responsibility, they contained some of the best moments of my life and the adjustment to another world was hard. I am grateful to Mr. Leech, for offering me a position in the alumnae office, which was located just across Walnut Grove in Moss Hall, but in reality, many miles away. In February 1980, I moved to the third floor of Greenwood Building and continued my work with alumnae and editing the "Alumnae News." In the fall of 1980, I made another move, this one to the main office, where I still worked with the alumnae, but also with the development office under Ann Copp, Director of Development.

Following Mr. Leech's retirement in January 1981, the Board again asked me to be Acting Head for the remainder of the school year. I worked closely with Virginia Pretti, Dean of the Upper School, and with Doris Bard, Business Manager, and her assistant, Bobbie Goforth. Somehow, we managed to survive the rest of the year. Geoffrey Butler, Assistant Headmaster of Louisville Collegiate School, accepted the position as St. Mary's Headmaster, arriving in July 1981. He encouraged me to stay in the development office, where I remained for the next seven years, enjoying my work with the directors, Ann Copp and Madge Clark.

In 1988, Mr. Southard, who was now Headmaster, suggested I move back to Moss Hall, where I continued working on *The St. Mary's News*, the archives, and my story of the school's 150 years. It has been a joy to work with Virginia Pretti and Kay Humphreys, Principals in the Lower School, to be friends with the teachers and staff, and to be around little children.

My thoughts are alive with memories—of the confidence placed in me by the headmasters, of the trust and encouragement of faculty and staff, of the support of the parents, and of my pride and joy in the students.

The years have passed quickly and now many of these girls I knew during my years as Dean are bringing their daughters to Moss Hall. These young faces speak to me of St. Mary's future generations holding fast to the standards that have made the school stand strong over so many years.

My dog, Maggie, has been my constant companion for eight years and attends school with me every day to the delight of the students. The children may not know who I am, but everyone knows Maggie, and they stop by my door to pet her. Sometimes they address me as "Maggie's Mom," or "that nice old lady." Those are my favorite titles.

Anne Fisher

In 1984, Geoffrey Butler asked Anne Fisher to be Dean of the Upper School, a position for which she had both the personal and professional qualities. Anne received a B.A. from Converse College in 1963, with a double major in Art History and English, and a M.S. in counseling from the University of Memphis. She accepted this position believing that "As Dean, I had the luxury of inheriting a highly successful program developed by my predecessors. The curriculum was in place, the faculty was superb, the Upper School office worked like a dream, and the students were busy and productive." Anne's understanding and sympathy for students and faculty was

*Anne Fisher, Upper School Dean
1984-1994:*

> *I saw my principal job as
> doing everything within my
> power to make it possible for
> the teachers to teach—to
> provide for the faculty the
> support, both physical and
> emotional—that was neces-
> sary to allow them to take
> care of the students.*

clearly evident. She made each one feel comfortable about coming to
her for counseling and for advice; she found the time to listen.
Besides being aware of the needs of others, she constantly reinforced
the high academic standards of the school.

Anne Fisher's first association with St. Mary's was in 1968, when
she was a parent searching for the best education for her daughter.
She showed her belief in the school even then: "I was certain I had a
brilliant child, so it seemed the only logical choice was St. Mary's."
Her daughter began junior Kindergarten that year, and Anne started
her own career at St. Mary's as an art history teacher. She continued
teaching for over fifteen years, sharing her passion for the visual
world with hundreds of students. In return, many of them had their
eyes opened to the world of art and also became passionate about
the subject. Alumnae often reminisce about her teaching and remark
that their trips to Europe were greatly enhanced by her class; many

Art teacher, Anne Fisher, 1969.

have given her the top accolade of choosing some form of art as a career. Enthusiasm by her students led to several parents and teachers asking to attend her class.

It was not long after her arrival at St. Mary's that Dr. Hughes recognized Anne's administrative ability. He asked her to develop a comprehensive summer program, incorporating the highly successful grammar and math classes required for entering students, adding a day camp, formulating an expanded academic program, and introducing classes in activities ranging from tennis to photography. In the summer of 1970, Anne and Mimi McCracken, Kindergarten teacher, welcomed seventeen campers. Five of these children were their own daughters. Under good leadership, small beginnings have a way of growing rapidly. The summer program was so successful that first year it quickly gained a reputation and grew in size each year. The day camp moved to the Moss Hall campus the summer of 1976 with over one hundred girls; the other programs, all co-educational, were still held on the main campus and continued to expand.

During the 1970s and 1980s, Anne added an art course for 7th and 8th graders and served as Student Council sponsor. Her many creative ideas gave the school an atmosphere it distinctly needed. As her Dean, I appreciated her support and encouragement, for she brought guidance and joy to my position; she could always be counted on not only to give her opinion frankly, but also to be supportive even in moments of disagreement. She opened my mind to many new ideas and especially made me realize the need for beauty in the school. Teachers like Anne make administrators appear to be better than they are.

In May 1991, St. Mary's was named a Blue Ribbon School by the United States Department of Education. This was the first time in three years that this prestigious academic honor had been won by a Memphis area school. This program recognizes academic excellence based on a detailed application and personal visits from a two-person team of educators. Tom Southard, Headmaster, said, "The award is significant because it represents recognition of academic excellence by educators at the highest level. I give credit for the award to Anne Fisher and the Upper School staff." Although this award was for the secondary school division, Mr. Southard also remarked, "The entire school deserves the honor." Mrs. Fisher was in total agreement: "We're very cognizant of the fact that this honor would not have been possible without the foundation the students

In the fall of 1991, Anne Fisher was the school's representative to the awards ceremony for the Blue Ribbon Schools in Washington, D.C.. Anne comments about the ceremony:

> *It was exciting being around representatives of other schools that had been worthy of this award. There was such diversity—from ten nuns running a school with 50 kids in Kentucky, to a school with over 2,900 students.*

Students plan a project with Mrs. Fisher.

receive at the lower grade levels. This is an honor for the entire school community."

In today's lingo, I can honestly say, that Anne was a workaholic. She worked many long hours, weekends included, and attended almost every function and activity of the school. Her concern and love for the students was clearly evident during her tenure. She honored the students by recognizing that "Their incredibly hard work needed to be balanced by a lot of fun."

She has fond memories of the creative things they did—the annual painting of the senior den (and the seniors as well), seniors singing (screaming) the alma mater at the Memphis International Airport as they awaited the English Speaking Union students, cross-country meets and soccer games and volleyball matches all over the county.

Anne made the students feel that she was a part of their lives, encouraging a variety of events such as a Halloween costume contest, for which she invariably came dressed as a witch, Light a Candle, the Christmas Pageant, the Faculty Band with Anne as the director (certainly creative, but perhaps not her most talented role), caravans to Fed Ex after midnight to load Christmas baskets, Father-Daughter dinner dances, Student Council election skits, and many others. She also admits, "Several things were only tolerated—Freshman Initiation, the Mr. Valentine contest with the Upper School office absolutely full of dozens of roses sent by high school boys and

A nne Fisher was and remains a powerful influence in both my professional and personal life. As a parent, teacher, an administrator, and a friend, Anne always lent her support and encouragement to her colleagues. I never felt that I worked for her; I always felt I worked with her. She helped me to understand young women, to expect the best from them, and to couple these high expectations with compassion.

—Faculty Member

college men, proms and 'after proms,' inappropriate chapel announcements, and Black Fridays."

Remarks by those who work for or with a person are apt to be true and honest statements, so I asked her secretaries to tell me their thoughts about "the real Anne." They quoted, as they had done once before, the French proverb: "Gratitude is the heart's memory." There were so many special memories: faculty, students, and alumnae coming by her office to talk with her and thank her for listening and counseling them; faculty being grateful for her hard work with the class schedule; Anne keeping open lines of communication with parents, students, and faculty; working long hours on a party for the seniors; hosting delightful faculty parties; making difficult jobs fun. One of her amazing traits, according to her secretaries, was her ability to do three things simultaneously. She could read a memo, talk on the phone, and write a letter all at the same time. They have a mental picture of her which they carry with them—glasses on top of her head, a big ring of keys, and a hot cup of tea overflowing with lemon.

Anne recalls that along with all the happy times during her years as Dean, there were hard times—especially the tragic and untimely deaths of mathematics teacher, Faith Leonard, and Betty Lou Stidham, Latin teacher. She realized and sympathized with the many setbacks of the students, both minor and major. Her constant faith in the girls is demonstrated in the following statement: "Perhaps especially in the darkest times—the students at St. Mary's always rose to the occasion in ways that made one proud to be a part of their young lives."

To the regret of all of us, Anne resigned her position as Dean in July 1994. As I write about her and other people's opinions of her, the thought reverberates in my mind that she gave of herself unstintingly. Her years at St. Mary's were spent holding high the academic standards of the school and emphasizing constant concern for the students and faculty.

Emily Matheny

Although it was 25 years ago, Emily Matheny still has vivid memories of her introduction to St. Mary's. At the request of Dr. Hughes, she came to the school to talk about coaching the varsity

Emily Matheny, Middle School Principal 1984-1990.

I was fortunate to be Dean of the Upper School when Emily began teaching at St. Mary's. I felt she was assigned to exactly the right age — 7th and 8th graders. She seemed to have an innate understanding of the adolescent girl; they quickly related to her, partially because of her youth and energy, but mostly because they realized her affection and high expectations for them.

tennis team. While touring the school, they went to the gym, and as she remembers it:

> I was young and spunky, so it seemed quite natural to me to pop a basketball up with my foot and put it through the net. I heard later from the faculty that he was partial to basketball players, especially blonde ones. Whether that was true or not, I do not know, but his gracious offer of a teaching position ... was a challenge I could not resist.

Emily graduated from Millsaps College in 1971, received her Master's degree from Memphis State in 1972, and began her teaching career at St. Mary's that fall. This was her first real teaching experience and not exactly what she had anticipated. She remembers, "My confidence quickly eroded when the best student in the eighth grade made 62 on my first test. Seeing her big tears was all I needed to convince me that I needed help quickly." She knew she was surrounded by many gifted educators and immediately asked for help from "these wonderfully seasoned teachers." It did not take her long to become skilled in her profession, for she was a quick study, immensely industrious, and constantly looking for ways to improve her skills.

In 1984, when the divisions of the school were changed, Emily was appointed Principal of the newly designed Middle School. It was believed eleven-twelve-and thirteen-year-old girls needed special attention and to have an identity of their own. The first year was a difficult one—especially for seventh and eighth graders who had anticipated being in the Upper School, but suddenly discovered they were still in Middle School.

Although in time, this proved to be a beneficial change, there was, naturally, a period of adjustment. This was the year that the "magic circles" were introduced to bring students and faculty together for a better understanding of each other. She realized the necessity of keeping them involved and busy and was their enthusiastic supporter.

As Emily talks about St. Mary's, she describes it as

> a place where everyone takes herself very seriously, striving earnestly to do the very best possible job at all times." Moments of sheer pleasure and foolishness are cherished. I remember the great delight the whole school took in choosing a mascot. We were in a league made up of small schools similar to St. Mary's. Since no one had any doubt

Fannie Warr and Andy Banks, loyal and longtime friends of the school.

Another never-to-be forgotten game was the year Fannie Warr, our beloved employee for 30 years, scored the winning bucket for the faculty/staff team. This was accomplished, as Emily expressed it, "on a last second 'Hail Mary' shot." The students were so excited about Fannie Warr's feat that they stampeded her with congratulatory hugs. It was a wonderful moment bringing faculty, students, and staff together, expressing love and appreciation for each other.

that SMS girls worked harder than all others combined, it seemed quite comical and healthy to be able to laugh at ourselves by acting like silly turkeys. Besides, serious students of history know that Ben Franklin had lobbied for the turkey to become a national bird. So the posters were made and the gobble calls practiced. Much to the delight of most and chagrin of some, the name has stuck for well over twenty years.

In her reflections, Emily emphasized that there was a good faculty/student relationship. They had respect for each other, partially due to the desire of almost all of the students to do well. Parents for the most part realized "the teachers could be trusted and wanted to help them achieve desired goals."

Each year there were faculty/student volleyball and basketball games which "were great spirit builders." By purchasing a ticket, students were allowed to wear jeans that day, which added to the popularity of the event. Emily remembers especially the year she was pregnant and could not play in the game. Instead, she was lady-in-waiting to the queen. It proved to be quite an uproarious occasion.

Chapel has played a significant role in Emily's life at St. Mary's. As she expressed it,

> Chapel was extremely important to my spiritual formation along with the personal relationships I still cherish with faculty, friends, students, and parents … The minutes spent praying, singing, listening, and worshiping as a community inside the church had a profound affect on my life, and, I believe, provided an essential part of the nurture necessary for the school to flourish. Just making time each day to be still and think about God became a discipline that has served me well.

She often reminded students, "When things are difficult at college you can take comfort in knowing that you are being prayed for each day back at St. Mary's."

Although Emily enjoyed her years at St. Mary's as an administrator, I believe that the most satisfying moments came when she was directly involved with the students in the classroom or taking a group of them on educational outings. Being a social studies teacher, she was especially delighted when students "enjoyed studying government or history."

*M*rs. Matheny was a very energetic teacher in that she was always trying to make her subject matter 'come alive.' I remember when we were studying about differences between forms of government, she arranged to ask Mr. Butler to visit the class and act like Hitler in order to demonstrate what a totalitarian system was like. She expected much from her students, and that helped us to be the best we could be.

—*One of Emily Matheny's Middle School Students*

The Reverend Emily Matheny after her graduation ceremony at Memphis Theological Seminary.

Emily is still involved with St. Mary's; her daughter, Claire, is a student. As a mother, she sees the school from another perspective and is most appreciative of all the care given to Claire by her teachers. She holds that this experience:

> has deepened the cherished memories of professional relationships and friendships during my days of active service at St. Mary's. These have graced my life since that ... long ago encounter with Dr. Hughes. They are part of the joy of a lifetime.

Emily's youth with all her enthusiastic ideas added a certain "joie de vivre" to the atmosphere of the school which was contagious. As her administrator for eight years, I realized it was invaluable to have a teacher "shake up" my thinking and question my ideas. My reactions to this were not always positive, but, at least it made me hesitate and re-think whatever issue was involved. For this I am greatly indebted to her. We all regretted Emily's leaving St. Mary's in 1990, but realized the seriousness of her call to the ministry. Her years here were a ministry to us. Working with her was part of the joy of my being an administrator.

7. MOSS HALL BECOMES A REALITY

David Leech

For the first time in the story of St. Mary's, an Episcopal priest was asked to be Headmaster of the school. The Reverend David Leech arrived in Memphis and at St. Mary's School in July 1974. Mr. Leech's successful experience in three independent schools with strong recommendations from each one indicated a promising future for him and for the school. It did not take long for me to realize the reasons for David Leech's success in his former schools. Almost immediately, I discovered he was efficient, careful in making decisions, and always kind. Although he was reserved, our relationship was a friendly one, and my respect for him grew steadily as we worked together. His memories for this book interested me greatly, for they revealed not only his thoughts about St. Mary's, but included much about himself and his past.

Mr. Leech was a product of the "Main Line" public schools of suburban Philadelphia. The Philadelphia schools had the reputation of being more rigorous and of having better college preparatory courses than the independent schools of that time. Because he attended these schools, it was not necessary for him to take college entrance examinations; certification from the high school principal was all that was needed for his college acceptance. He attended the College of Arts and Sciences at the University of Pennsylvania and between 1941 and 1945 earned the following three degrees: B.A. in English, B.S. in Library Science, and M.A. in Anthropology. In 1946,

The Reverend David Leech.

he was interested in teaching at an Ivy League school, but to his surprise, he discovered these colleges paid their young staff in accord with the school's prestigious reputation, rather than with an adequate salary. He felt this was unsatisfactory and accepted a position as chief librarian of Roanoke College in Virginia, where he taught English and anthropology in alternate years and worked hard to modernize a Victorian library. As he undertook his labors, he discovered, "Many books were actually devoured by book worms, the real things!"

In 1948, Mr. Leech began his studies for the priesthood of the Episcopal Church, paying his way by working in the seminary library. Here, he studied Greek and became a New Testament scholar. After ordination and graduation, his first position was as a

*I*n 1974, when I first visited
St. Mary's, I knew 'the fit
was tight,' but the beauty of
the new Upper School building made the greatest impression on me and the great
need for more school space
did not hit me until I arrived.
—David Leech

priest in Bucks County, Pennsylvania, where he thoroughly enjoyed
a life oriented toward preaching and teaching young people. He met
and married an English/Canadian girl, Doris Edna Brown, and it was
their mutual decision that he accept the offer of the chaplaincy of St.
Andrew's School in Middletown, Delaware. Here he entered a world
in the 1950s that could have been the year 1350: "All boys, all men,
church, daily chapel, sacred studies, sung services, plus athletics, as
the muscular Christianity of the late Victorians."

Mr. Leech's next move was to Huntsville, Alabama, where there
was an interest in establishing an independent school of quality as
an alternative to the public schools of a traditional southern city. It
was an excellent choice, for during these years, Huntsville proved to
be an exciting community with the influx of the "rocket people,"
including Von Braun's successful German rocket engineers and their
families. He became the founding Headmaster of The Randolph
School, which developed under his tenure into a tremendously successful independent school. He remained with this school for eight
years before moving to Oregon in 1967, where he was asked to
become the head of the large and ancient schools of the Diocese of
Oregon in Portland. There were three schools in Portland: a six-
grade coed day school, a girl's seventh through twelfth day and
boarding school, and a new boy's seventh through twelfth day and
boarding school. To pull these three schools together was a challenge and resulted in a huge task for three main reasons: boarding
schools at this time were falling out of favor, the so-called coordinate
school's concept rose and fell, and the California drug dealers discovered Oregon to be an untapped virgin market for students. In
spite of these obstacles, Mr. Leech managed successfully to merge
two middle and Upper Schools, one for girls, one for boys, and created one co-ed boarding and day school, all with a new name:
Oregon Episcopal School. For a time, he was vice-president and
president-elect of the Northwest Association of Independent Schools.

He also was impressed with "the skill, the hard work, the utter
devotion of the St. Mary's faculty." He quotes one truck line as
advertising, "Our driving force is our people." He believed this could
be said of the school's faculty.

Shortcomings in the facilities of the school made Mr. Leech
realize it was necessary "to walk carefully with the host church." He
mentions how gracious both the Rector, Harold Barrett, and his wife

Mr. Leech became good friends with Mr. Moss and described him as "a sagacious old man." True wisdom and foresight was shown by Mr. Leech in realizing that this property would answer some of St. Mary's pressing needs: space for more buildings, room for a burgeoning Lower School, a playground, and a gymnasium. Because of Mr. Leech's wisdom and vision, these additions have all come into existence, and every inch of the space is used daily.

Mr. Leech's vision to purchase Moss Hall (pictured right) was an invaluable contribution to the school.

were in their South Carolina ways, but soon knew because of the scarcity of space, the school would have to withdraw from some of the daily use of the church buildings, "if we were to remain as happy co-owners of the facilities." Mr. Leech quickly realized that the beautiful church building was a tremendous asset to the school and few churches would show the hospitality that the Church of the Holy Communion had given to St. Mary's. One of the reasons Mr. Leech felt he had been chosen for this position was that he, an Episcopal priest, and Harold Barrett, the Rector of Holy Communion, "could co-exist peacefully together."

The endless details of assessing faculty needs, acquiring property, designing facilities, or even harder, redesigning facilities and raising funds, took a great deal of his time away from being the academic head he had hoped to be and as he had been in Huntsville. It was more like the facilities/fund raising head that he had been in Oregon. It was fortuitous that the Morrie Moss property was available for purchase in 1975. His vision to purchase the Moss Hall property was an invaluable contribution to the school and has been one of the main reasons for St. Mary's development during the past twenty-one years. John Cawthon, Chairman of the Board of Trustees, announced, "It was a generous contribution from Mr. and Mrs. Moss." The property was valued at $438,000 and sold to St. Mary's for $200,000. The

When Mr. Leech first tried introducing computers into the curriculum in 1979, he was amused at the responses of some of the faculty who claimed that it was "a trade school subject." At the time, his suggestion was that the course be a second semester senior elective. His foresight introduced St. Mary's to the technological age. Currently, St. Mary's employs six computer instructors and owns approximately 250 computers.

Charles Curtiss, Plant Manager 1976-1996. "A man for all seasons."

residence containing eighteen rooms was built initially in 1950 and enlarged in 1963. Mr. Leech remarked at the time, "The Moss Hall property means ... flexibility and the chance to do even better work with girls, something we have been doing for 128 years."

He also realized the need for a Development Office which opened in 1979 with Ann Humphreys Copp '64 as Director. It was essential that the endowment of the school be increased to help defray the cost of educating students, to improve faculty salaries and to raise money for scholarships. Development began as a one-woman office but soon developed to encompass admissions, the annual fund, alumnae, and public relations.

Several new programs were initiated by Mr. Leech. One was the organization of a band. Orchestral music was actually his love, but the beginning of a small "athletic band" opened the door to having a larger band and a band leader. A few people did not agree; one mother remarked, "It is not ladylike to play a band instrument." This band has grown tremendously since its inception and has become a very important part of the school. This program has brought about the discovery of many talented students and has added another dimension to the entire school.

During Mr. Leech's years at St. Mary's, the school continued to grow, not as much in size but in facilities and the offering of new programs. The divisions of the school were changed. By 1976, the Lower School, grades Kindergarten through third with Katharine Phillips, Principal, was now on the beautiful Moss Hall property; Middle School, four through six was with Camille Deaderick, Principal; the Upper School remained the same, grades seven through twelve, and I continued as Dean.

As Mr. Leech is remembered at St. Mary's, certain definite characteristics surface. The faculty remembers his wit, his precise, impressive vocabulary, and his erudite speeches. His announcements in chapel demonstrated a masterful command of the English language. One faculty member still mentions his beautiful handwriting and his penchant for neatness. His desk reminded one of the perfect order found on a surgeon's tray, everything exactly where it should be. He took a torn piece of paper out of the Dean Virginia Pretti's hand one day and cut it carefully with a pair of scissors. He was teased about this neatness frequently, but always affectionately, and his response was good-natured.

Molly Townes, Student Council President, presents Mr. Leech with the council's gift to the school on Class Day, May 1977.

Mr. Leech's respect for female teachers and administrators was constantly evident, and some of his thoughts were revealed in an article in The Press/Scimitar. *An excerpt from that article is as follows:*

Women have Kept
St. Mary's Alive.
St. Mary's exists today because women wanted it to. St. Mary's has existed in a miraculous manner, to meet threats against its existence ...
It has weathered all the different storms, thanks to a small number of women who had enough foresight to realize the school's potential for progress.

He wanted to be a Headmaster along the role of a "Mr. Chips"; he believed "teachers and administrators should consider their positions a calling rather than an opportunity to receive a salary commensurate with their worth."

Those of us in chapel in 1975 will never forget the day Mr. Leech wore a kilt and announced that students were now allowed to wear pants to school. He received a standing ovation—first of all, for allowing pants as part of the dress code, and second, for having the courage to wear the kilt. The excitement continued throughout the day, and from that moment, there was no question he was a man attuned to the change in women's attire. Blue jeans, however, were still not allowed—except on special days.

According to Mr. Leech, the school was "academically conservative" and met all the necessary requirements for entrance to fine colleges. Actually, Mr. Leech believed "the Upper School is more like a liberal arts college than an American high school." Indeed, the school has an excellent scholarship program that stresses academics. Mr. Leech also mentioned, "When I was in college, boys had many more opportunities for leadership than girls." At St. Mary's, he became aware of one of the definite advantages of a single sex school for girls as the school with its standards and ideals offers them the opportunity to become outstanding women. Although St. Mary's is an Episcopal School, Mr. Leech believes that "It has also maintained an ecumenical aim throughout its history; the daily chapel service continues and is an important component of the school's structure."

As in the past, students were administered an admission test during the Leech tenure and approved by an admissions committee on the basis of this test and their past academic records. In 1975, tuition ranged from $700 in Kindergarten to $1500 for the Upper School. Mr. Leech emphasized his philosophy towards faculty:

> Faculty members are allowed independence in teaching. They are not given a lot of guidelines which allows a fresh attitude and approach in teaching. No attempt is made to typecast faculty members. In 1979, the school employed 69 teachers, of whom, 45% had advanced degrees. [Also the school] has adopted an educational program for faculty that finances faculty continuing education programs.

During his years at St. Mary's, there were several very sad and difficult days for both St. Mary's and Mr. Leech. At the very beginning of his first school year, the Director of the Kindergarten, Mignon Payne, died tragically and suddenly of cancer. It was a tragedy and loss to the school and also for Mr. Leech to lose such a fine, outstanding Kindergarten Director.

In 1976, his wife, Doris, died unexpectedly, making another very sad time for him and the school. He demonstrated both his character and his courage through his unswerving dedication despite his personal feelings. When Mr. Leech retired from St. Mary's in 1981, the total enrollment was around 700. In a letter to friends of the St. Mary's community, he praised St. Mary's, its students, and faculty members and said he "could not imagine a better last assignment as a Headmaster." For several years, he worked in development at a college in Michigan. In his *Memoirs*, he reveals that he met many fascinating and wonderful people during his years at St. Mary's. He feels fortunate to be able to say, "I grew during this time." As he states it, "I regretted parting from so many wonderful Memphis people." In the long run, however, he did not regret leaving, for he walked into a position for which he was uniquely qualified and thoroughly enjoyed.

Mr. Leech was a good friend as well as a fine Headmaster and will long be remembered for his intelligence, his vision for St. Mary's, and the many improvements for which he was responsible. He, along with his predecessors, believed in the philosophy of the school, and he was dedicated to holding the threads together so evident throughout St. Mary's long history.

The following is a quotation from Mr. Leech's letter to friends and parents of the school as he left St. Mary's:
St. Mary's is a singularly blessed school. It is better to have served St. Mary's than a dozen lesser schools. It has been a rewarding challenge to me to maintain the quality of the school I was asked to lead, to work to make a fine school even better.

Madelyn Brock

One of the thoughts that has come to me often while writing this book is that there have been people connected with the school for a short time who have literally been "life-savers." This title could be easily be applied to Madelyn Brock. Madelyn was a graduate of Mary Baldwin College, and had experience teaching Kindergarten at Rouhlac's Kindergarten before becoming Director of Physical Education at Southwestern (now Rhodes College).

Kindergarten teachers at Moss Hall: (left to right) Sue Williams, Madelyn Brock, Acting Principal, Sydney Bates, Betty Lyon, and Mimi McCracken.

In 1975, Madelyn accepted a position at St. Mary's. Although the Kindergarten did not have a Director after Mignon Payne's death in 1974, an excellent group of Kindergarten teachers successfully ran this division of the school. There was a need, however, for another teacher, and the addition of Madelyn Brock was a welcome one. The Kindergarten moved to Moss Hall in 1976 with Katharine Phillips as Principal of the Lower School. At the time of Katharine's retirement in 1981, Madelyn was asked to be Interim Principal for the 1980-81 school year as well as to teach Kindergarten. She continued this working position through the 1981-1982 school year with the proviso that her responsibility would be limited to being Interim Principal.

Her desire to resign at the end of 1982 was accepted with sadness, for, as a person and as a teacher, her presence at the school was invaluable. To show the school's love and respect for her, she

Madelyn thoroughly enjoyed interacting with the students. If you could not locate her immediately, the teachers would often look under the viaduct where she might be playing Billy Goat Gruff with the girls. One Halloween, she was found sitting on a bale of hay in a wonderful witch costume that failed to frighten the girls; instead it delighted them.

was awarded the honor of being Outstanding Teacher in 1982. One of the Lower School teachers noted, "Children will miss her hugs, and special ways of dissolving tears into smiles; parents, her willingness to listen; and teachers, her leadership and support." One of her students affectionately dubbed her "Miss Broccoli," another student showed her feelings by asking "What's green and funny and lives at Moss Hall? Mrs. Broccoli." Her efficiency and her graciousness in taking over the role of Interim Kindergarten Principal when the school needed her will be remembered as a generous gift to St. Mary's.

Camille Deaderick

A native Arkansan, Lady Camille Deaderick came to Memphis to attend Southwestern where she graduated with a B.A. degree and a year later received an M.A. from the University of Memphis in elementary education and counseling. She taught in a variety of positions in elementary schools for eleven years—Wells Station Elementary School, Grace St. Luke's, and Miss Hutchison's School. At this point in her life, she decided to leave the world of little children to try the college scene again, accepting a position at her alma mater, Southwestern. In 1976, she answered a call to teach second grade at St. Mary's Moss Hall. One of the memories of her first year was finding her classroom empty and all the students on the roof; they were known as the spirited class of '88—always ready for an adventure.

At the request of Mr. Leech, Camille became Principal of the Middle School in 1978, which then consisted of grades four, five, and six. There was a need for the Middle School to develop a program more appropriate for this age. At her suggestion, peer counseling began with the class of '88. The students were divided into small groups to interact with each other and give them an opportunity to develop better relationships. The science department instigated an important change in the program— requiring all work on science projects be completed at the school. Many fun field trips were initiated—a very popular one was to a cotton patch in Arkansas. Another project initiated during these years was the opening of a bookstore for the middle school to give the students an opportunity to develop responsibility. Intramural soccer was also introduced in the Middle

Camille Deaderick, Middle School Principal, with her students: (left to right) Elizabeth Owen, Kathryn Haggitt, Leslie Martin, Susan Holloway, Jean Vaughan, and Traci Sherman.

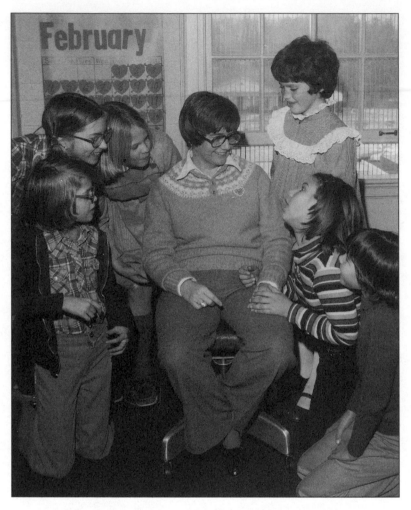

School. It caught on immediately and is one of the most popular sports for that age.

In 1984-85, Camille decided to resign her position as Principal and return to full time teaching, moving back to the Lower School; again she taught second grade. Her Principal describes her as having a warm toughness—no nonsense in her class, but always willing to go the extra mile. A strong advocate of high academic standards, she believes in single sex schools for girls, as girls seem to perform at a higher level if they are not in a classroom with boys and continually concerned with their appearance. She embraces the Episcopal form of religion, for it instills in girls a broad view of religion and does not enclose them within narrow limits; it allows diverse opinions in their religious lives. One of her most important tasks has been organizing the chapel program for the Lower School. It now has more of an Episcopal orientation and flavor.

In 1990 at the commencement exercises, she was awarded the honor of Outstanding Teacher for her many contributions to St. Mary's. An article written about her noted that her classroom has been described as "a buzz of controlled activity" and that "students respond to her direct, straight-forward approach to learning … There's no falling asleep in her class—she's known for re-charging brains." Besides her positions as teacher and Principal, she has been a hard-working member of several committees.

The very difficult and frustrating position of organizing the car-pool regime was delegated to her several years ago. As a result, along with the assistance of the other teachers, it is efficiently run. One student's mother asked her daughter, "What does 'Miss D' teach?" The student very quickly responded, "She doesn't teach; she is in charge of the cars and parking."

Camille is also known as a "grammar guru" and epitomizes "tough love." The students affectionately nicknamed her "Miss D" or "Miss Dee" long ago, and the name has stuck ever since. Her principal and her associates emphasize her organizational ability, her devotion to her girls, and her dedication to St. Mary's.

Virginia Pretti

My first contact with Virginia Pretti was at a Memphis Association of Independent Schools' meeting. At the time, she was Headmistress of St. Agnes Academy; instantly, I liked her. She was open, friendly, and frank. Her remarks were to the point, accompanied always by her quick wit and delightful sense of humor, adding spice and enjoyment to the meetings. At that time, there were very few schools belonging to the Memphis Association of Independent Schools, so we had an opportunity to talk and to become friends.

Virginia received her B.A. degree in English at Siena College, her M.A. in Administration and Supervision from Memphis State University, and worked in education for twenty years as a teacher, guidance counselor, and principal. She began her career teaching at St. Dominic's School for Boys for three years before moving to St. Agnes. In 1965, she left the private school to become a part of a new federally funded program for disadvantaged children in the Memphis

Virginia Pretti, Upper School Dean 1979-1984.

City Schools and began work on an advanced degree in school psychology. Following that year, she had the experience of teaching emotionally disturbed children in a semi-boarding situation. In 1968, she returned to St. Agnes as the first lay principal of grades one through twelve, and remained there for ten years.

As I heard the news that Virginia Pretti had resigned from St. Agnes to become a home builder with two former teachers, I thought immediately she would be the perfect candidate for the position of Dean of St. Mary's Upper School.

I have thought and remarked many times that helping to convince her was probably my best contribution to St. Mary's.

Virginia began her work here in January 1979, and it was soon evident that she was an excellent choice for this position. Her organizational ability was needed and quickly recognized. In 1981, David Leech resigned, and I became Acting Headmistress of the school. This gave us an opportunity to work even more closely together. I became more and more convinced of her talent as a leader.

Virginia told me when she accepted the position as Dean of the Upper School that she would stay until St. Mary's found my replacement—about a year and a half. Nineteen years have passed and she's still here. She insists:

> I truly believed that my time at St. Mary's would be short. I hadn't really changed jobs many times but there was always a willingness to move on when an interesting challenge presented itself. From the day I was introduced to the student body in chapel, I felt something different. The chapel service was so impressive and warm. Something seemed to take hold of me that day and I knew that this was where I would work until retirement. St. Mary's combines a superior academic program with high personal standards and unparalleled concern for each student. The faculty is incredible, open, and are the kind of people with whom you love to spend time.

Virginia served as the Dean of the Upper School for five years. Maintaining the academic standards and the integrity of the Honor system were her priorities. At a time when it was popular for schools to offer a smorgasbord of courses, Virginia and the faculty held fast

Students Cindy Willmott, Molly McCarroll, Lisa Jaeger (class of '81), Joan Daniel, English teacher, Kathi Welch, and Edie Kang (class of '80).

Mary Greer Simonton, with her Principal, Miss Pretti.

Ballerina Rachel White with Miss Pretti.

to rigorous requirements for graduation and to a curriculum confined to the essentials of an outstanding college preparatory program. To ensure that students had the opportunity to develop solid study skills, Virginia devised Supervised Study, or "SS," as the students called it. Time after time students discovered that two hours of organized and focused work helped them develop strong study skills and they could complete their work in a reasonable length of time. Working hard, playing hard, and having fun were all part of the Upper School experience. Virginia spent the night at school during Freshmen Initiation, found ways to keep the seniors in check on Black Friday, attended games, plays, dances, and fund raisers—all opportunities to become involved with the students on a personal level. One of Virginia's secretaries, Betty Jane Barringer, gave some insight into her character.

> She is one of those rare people who deep inside is good. The students were always her first priority; the faculty came next; she was straight forward and direct; didn't mince words; she told it like it was. Virginia had a well-known gesture; when she put her hand on my elbow and said, 'Let's go get a ...' I knew something was up. [This gesture is still known by all her teachers and staff.] Her leadership style was such that she would present an idea, drop it, move to another topic. By the end of the discussion, however, the idea that she had originally proposed had become my idea and I was 100% in favor of whatever it was ... She didn't waste time nor did she waste others' time. Meetings ran smoothly. She didn't allow anyone to monopolize the discussion. Virginia was able to delegate authority effectively, bringing out the best in those around her and she made us laugh a lot. A uniquely wonderful person, educator, and friend.

In 1984, the Lower School at Moss Hall was very much in need of a principal. Also, the Lower School was not accredited by The Southern Association of Secondary Schools and Colleges; Geoff Butler, Headmaster, realized this was necessary, and to accomplish this, the school needed experienced and strong leadership. Realizing her gift in this direction, Geoff appointed Virginia as Principal of the Lower School and K-12 Curriculum Coordinator. As he stated, "Ms. Pretti's breadth of knowledge and leadership stature with faculty at all levels gave her a unique authority to coordinate the entire curriculum throughout the grades." Her performance as Dean of the

Miss Pretti is welcomed to Moss Hall as Lower School Principal in 1984.

Upper School was outstanding and the teachers and students regretted losing her, but the Lower School was delighted. In her words:

> Leaving the Upper School was one of the hardest decisions I ever made; however, I felt it would be better to oversee the curriculum if I were on the Lower School campus. I had the advantage of already knowing many of the teachers and immediately fell in love with 200 somewhat toothless children.

As she talks about the Lower School, she readily admits:

> It captivated my heart. I had to quickly learn about Carebears, carpool lines, the Christmas Pageant, and the Lower School lingo... I found working on the curriculum was an all-consuming chore. A Character Education Program was developed by the faculty that combines the development of virtues and the development of community responsibility. Friday morning assembly is devoted to the exploration of virtues and moral behaviors.

Children instinctively know she cares about them. They delight in her sense of humor and react joyfully to the spirit of fun, which is such a part of her nature. As in her Upper School involvement, she takes part in many of their school activities. Virginia substitutes when needed, visits their classrooms, and roller skates with them. She has a bulletin board on her office door on which students may leave messages or requests to see her. Very seldom is there any

Almost everyone has something to say about Virginia Pretti, especially her teachers. One remarked:

> *She likes the challenge of a problem and is excellent at solving it. When she makes a decision, I always feel that she is listening to everyone and takes time to arrive at a consensus. She tries very hard to be fair and invariably has the best interest of the children at heart.*

Students on a field trip with Miss Pretti.

misbehavior in her presence. She demands their respect without losing their affection.

Comments from a teacher reveal, "She is always game for a skit; she is a ham at heart and seems to enjoy every bit of it." One problem the teachers have is that "she is forever changing the cafeteria routine just when we have all gotten used to it— even down to placing or replacing the trash cans." As this plainly demonstrates, she tends to be detail oriented, which is perhaps one reason the Lower School is so well organized. On the other hand, according to another member of her faculty:

> She just sort of jumps out of any box one might try to put her in. She is a person of great contrasts and seeming contradictions … One of the qualities I appreciate most about working with Virginia is her commitment to the spirit of the law, rather than a rigid adherence to the letter of the law. She is no stranger to self-criticism and does not expect personal perfection from others. Hard work, dedication, intelligence and lots of my time, but not perfection.

Mainly, because of her leadership, the Lower School has grown from 150 students to its present enrollment of 400. This is important, but not as important as the many programs she has added, the faculty that she selects very carefully, and the joyous atmosphere of the school she has created. A spirit of camaraderie and cooperation is evident, making Moss Hall a wonderful place to work.

8. DEVELOPMENT AND DIVERSITY

Geoffrey C. Butler

The eighties saw many changes in administration and programs along with the addition of Hyde Building to the Moss Hall campus. Technology increased from one computer in the development office to computers in every office and classroom. The library began its progress towards being a modern information center. Computers were used by the library and were connected through Maislic with other independent schools in Memphis. More emphasis was placed on development, and the school had its first full-time directors of admissions and alumnae. Because of its wise leadership and fine teachers, St. Mary's continued its reputation as an outstanding college preparatory school.

Mr. Geoffrey C. Butler, Headmaster from 1981-1987, was a strong believer in the academic emphasis at St. Mary's. A graduate of Washington and Lee University, he received his M.A. in history from Trinity College in Hartford, Connecticut. He began his career in 1966 at Suffield Academy and held various posts at that school before joining the Louisville Collegiate School in Louisville, Kentucky, in 1975 as Assistant Headmaster. When he and his wife, Evelyn Lee Day Butler, a former Memphian, and their three sons came to Memphis, Robert F. Fogelman, Chairman of the Board of Trustees, announced:

> The appointment of Mr. Butler ends a long and careful search for the individual we feel can best carry on the academic standards and traditions that have helped build St. Mary's outstanding reputation among girls' school in the United States.

Geoffrey C. Butler, Headmaster 1981-1987.

Along with the faculty and administration, I remember Geoff Butler's first talk to the school. He said, "I love God; I love my church; I love my wife; I love my children; I love to fish; I love to work in a school." It was a most unusual, but effective beginning. The faculty was impressed immediately with his enthusiasm and his vitality, and so were the students, because he knew their names. A member of the office staff said that as soon as he arrived in Memphis, he started studying the Carillon, *the school's yearbook, to learn the names of the students. By the opening of school, he could call almost every Upper School student by her name.*

In an article written recently, entitled "St. Mary's Remembered," Mr. Butler talks about his first impressions:

I found an extraordinary community of teachers and students who worked hard, achieved much and cared deeply for one another. St. Mary's faculty and students held long established reputations for strength, courage and independence that far preceded the women's liberation movement … That heritage was then, and remains forever, the core of St. Mary's.

He continued his remarks by emphasizing:

St. Mary's strong academic program, deep and worthwhile traditions, genuine religious conviction, dedicated faculty

The Reverend Reynolds Cheney, Rector, Church of the Holy Communion.

Father Cheney reminded me that they were involved in another athletic pursuit. The two of them occasionally took time away from their respective institutions to play tennis, and Geoff had a hard time believing an 'older man' could play such good tennis.

and bright, alert girls ... The commitment of time for chapel each day gave the girls [an opportunity] to worship and reflect as a school community ... [It] made a clear and unmistakable statement about the importance of worship in individual and corporate life.

The Reverend Reynolds Cheney, Rector of the Church of the Holy Communion, and Mr. Butler came to Memphis the same year, and Geoff remarked:

We created a unique opportunity to reassert a cooperative relationship ... [and] we agreed to support mutually the needs and work of both the church and the school ... Father Cheney took an interest in the school chapel program, attended school events, and even lent his considerable frame to the faculty volleyball team in its contest with the girls.

Besides Geoff's close association with Reynolds Cheney, he felt the school was helped by parishioners of the Church of the Holy Communion, many of whose children were students at St. Mary's and others who were supportive of the 'joint mission of the school and the church.' Among them were Harry Schadt, Arthur Best, Newton Allen, Louis Haglund, Al Whitman, Warren Cruzen, Rich Wilson, Jack Bolton, Charles Crump, Bob McRae, Jim Fri, Jack Gordon, Roy Bell, Jack Thurmond, Jim and Sally Barksdale, Pete Willmott, Bonnie Smith, Eric Muirhead, Fred and Harriette Beeson, Cynthia Pitcock, John McQuiston, Huey Holden, Ben Ward, Walker Uhlhorn, Bill Vaughan, Jim Warner, and Tricia Dudley. These hard-working people, along with countless others, labored to provide facilities and other resources that benefitted both the school and the church.

It was not long before we discovered that Geoff was a great believer in retreats. Although St. Mary's was already a close community, Geoff felt it would help create opportunities "to strengthen communications and bonds among students and faculty. Hence was born the idea of the infamous faculty retreat in 1982 ...." It was held at the Walt's Country Place, and the faculty cooperated, "some willingly, some reluctantly."

In retrospect, Geoff remarked, "Perhaps the greatest force for unifying the faculty out of this experience was their suspicion of the new Headmaster who made them participate. Though useful in providing faculty with a chance to come together, this proved to be a one-time event."

*Geoffrey Butler at the
student retreat.*

*It seems to me that Geoff had
a call to life in the wilderness.
I remember one summer that
he even had his own retreat.
He journeyed to the moun-
tains of Colorado or some-
where in the vast regions of
the west for a few weeks—
away from work and family.
He returned with many wonderful stories about his experiences and surprised us with
a new look. He was on the
retreat long enough to return
as "the bearded Headmaster."
The question Reynolds
Cheney and the school pon-
dered was, "Did he violate the
dress code?"*

Another retreat was initiated for the students which was more successful. It included leaders from all activities who spent a weekend each fall discussing student issues of concern for the coming school year. A senior retreat was also established to give students an opportunity to reflect on their experiences at St. Mary's and "preview the expectations and changes of approaching college life." Also, the seventh grade was involved in a retreat at Camp Hy-Lake in East Tennessee, where they learned about taking care of themselves in the out-of-doors.

In the fall of 1984, Geoff made several very important administrative changes. The Lower School needed a new administrator, and he remembered a conversation with Virginia Pretti in which she jokingly had mentioned she would like the position of Principal of the Lower School when she retired. Little did she realize that this would occur long before her retirement. Unfortunately the situation at Moss Hall during the 1982-84 school years was not a happy one for either the school or for Mary Williams, Principal. Morale was deteriorating, and after Mary Williams' resignation, the Lower School needed a skilled and experienced head. In 1984-85, Geoff offered her the position of Principal, along with the position of Assistant Head for Academic Affairs. This necessitated another change. When Miss Pretti relinquished her position, Anne Fisher was appointed Dean of the Upper School. Emily Matheny remained as Principal of the Middle

School, at that time grades five through eight. Geoff referred to these three—Pretti, Fisher, and Matheny as the "unholy trinity." According to him, they truly ran the educational program of the school for the remainder of his tenure.

Ann Copp, Director of Development, 1980-1986, worked very closely with Geoff. Both being new in their particular positions, they depended on each other and developed a trust relationship which served St. Mary's well. Ann described Geoff as "straight forward, supportive, open-minded, a person of integrity and compassion. His sense of humor often made difficult situations liveable and created moments of companionship and catharsis." Ann was impressed with how hard Geoff worked. He arrived early and left late, and the few times she was at the school on Saturday, he was always there. It amazed Ann that

> although Geoff was the father of three sons, his respect for women was unerring. His enthusiasm grew from an apparently firm conviction that our planet would be a better place if we listened to its women who had the self-esteem, courage and skills to speak with conviction and persistence … He was proud to be associated with St. Mary's.

Madge Clark, Director of the Annual Fund, followed Ann Copp as Director of Development and gives Ann credit "for enabling our program to achieve much of the success that we enjoyed in the years I was there." According to Madge:

> My thoughts about Geoff Butler swirl around what a pleasure it was to serve on his administrative team, first as part-time coordinator of the Annual Fund, then as full-time Director of Development. He asked me to be his eyes and ears and tell him the good and the bad about the school and about him. This charge made me feel truly trusted, highly valued, and vital to him … Geoff and I wrote the Case Statement for our first big Capital Campaign together. The process was fun, challenging, and successful, for we, along with the assistance of the Board of Trustees, were successful in raising money for construction of the Moss Hall addition … and the Margaret Hyde Activities Center, [in additon to increasing] … the Endowment Fund.

One of Geoff Butler's many contributions was his emphasis on diversity of the student body. The following statement emphasizes this thought: "It is my impression that St. Mary's makes a genuine effort to attract students from diverse elements within Memphis, and it is my intention to continue to build upon this foundation." In an article he wrote for the *Tri-State Defender*, he clearly gave his opinion on this subject:

> We are involved not only in equipping our students to be successful academically, but more importantly to be successful human beings. In the more pluralistic society in which our children will live, they must be taught not only to tolerate difference, but to appreciate the richness of diversity. As the Episcopal Schools report states, 'No matter what the content of education may be, the process of education is enhanced through the diversity which students and teachers bring to it. Dialogue, not monologue, fosters learning.'

He was also a believer in the single sex school for girls as revealed by this statement: "I remain convinced that in the single sex environment we have a special opportunity to encourage a drive for excellence and to nurture a large measure of true confidence built on achievement." He was a believer in building self-esteem in girls, in giving girls early training in leadership skills, and helping them deal constructively with the stresses presented by parents, school, and friends, as well as the physical and emotional changes of adolescence.

Improvements were made to the existing school and plans were made for future additions during Geoff's tenure as Headmaster. Barth Building was renovated in 1984 with the addition of Anne's Room, dedicated to Anne Garrett '79 and donated by her parents, Drs. Edward and Christine Garrett. This room has been used in a variety of ways—for Upper School seminar classes, many after-school meetings, and also by the church for vestry meetings. The Board of Trustees in 1986-87 realized the need to enlarge and expand school facilities for larger classes in the Lower School, which would, in time, mean an explosion of students for the Middle and Upper Schools. Also, there was a need to provide more athletic and activity space for the entire school. It was during this year that architectural plans were created which later became the Margaret Hyde Activity Center on the Moss Hall campus.

Geoff was recognized for his ability as an administrator not only at St. Mary's but also in Memphis and at the State of Tennessee. He was elected President of the Tennessee Association of Independent Schools for 1986-87, served on the Commission on Excellence in

Geoff's remembrances about St. Mary's reveal his appreciation of his years at the school:

The accumulation of daily companionship with the wonderful faculty and children blends into a unique wholeness. One public event stands out in my memory as a particularly clear moment. On the occasion of the graduation of the one hundredth graduating class (in the school's 137-year history) in 1985, the graduation ceremony returned to St. Mary's Cathedral. The presence with the martyrs of Memphis, the Sisters of St. Mary's, whose names are carved in the chancel steps, and the witness to the graduation of another generation of St. Mary's girls recaptured the strength of heritage and the hope of faith.

Education for the Memphis City Schools, was a member of the Committee on Education for the Memphis Jobs Conference, served on the Board of Directors of the Youth Concert Ballet, and was a member of the Vestry of Holy Communion Episcopal Church.

Geoff resigned in 1987 to accept a position at Fort Worth Country Day School in Fort Worth, Texas. His decision to leave was a difficult one for St. Mary's to accept. We admired his respect for his associates and the students and his willingness to listen and to learn. His vitality and his refreshing sense of humor revived many of us during long meetings and difficult moments. Although I was aware of his accomplishments while he was here, writing about them has made me realize more and more how much St. Mary's benefitted from his years with us.

Geoffrey C. Butler, Headmaster, at Baccalaureate, May 1987: (left to right) Ruth Cheney, Gwynne Keathley, Gail Borod, and Janie Barnett.

Kay Humphreys

In 1981, Kay Humphreys applied for the position of Kindergarten teacher. At that time, I was Acting Headmistress and had the pleasure of interviewing her. I remember talking with her and thinking she is someone we would love to have on our faculty. Kay's first interest in St. Mary's began after meeting Mignon Payne in 1966, who, she felt, ran a most impressive Kindergarten program. She continued to be in touch with Mignon through their years of association with the Memphis Kindergarten Study Group.

Kay Humphreys, Director of St. Mary's Kindergarten, 1992 to present.

Kay graduated from the University of Tennessee at Martin in Home Economics, majoring in Child Development and worked in the Early Childhood Center while in college. Her M.S. degree was received from Memphis State University in 1981. In the sixties, she was a Case Worker and then a Licensing Counselor for the Tennessee Department of Human Services, a position which she held for the second time after being a Trainer in the Head Start program for two summers. From 1979-1981, she taught at the University Churches Pre-School and Day Care Center, coming to St. Mary's in the fall of 1981. She taught various sections of the Kindergarten until the spring of 1992. Her skill as Kindergarten teacher and her obvious administrative ability led to her being appointed Kindergarten Director as well as continuing to teach in the classroom. In the fall of 1992, she became full-time Director of the Kindergarten Program, but even after five years, she still misses being in the classroom. She is married to Dr. Mel Humphreys, a professor at the University of Memphis, and they have two sons and two grandsons.

During Geoffrey Butler's tenure, the Kindergarten changed to being a four-hour daily program, and Extended Day was offered from 12:00-3:00. The girls in this program called it "Splendid Day." Soon, there was such a demand for both Junior and Senior Kindergarten that an additional section was added. Many parents also showed interest in a class for girls with late summer or early fall birthdays, so our first Pre-Kindergarten class for girls age 3 1/2, was initiated under Kay. This program met in the afternoons four times a week; in the first year, there were 13 girls. At the present time, there are two sections of Pre-Kindergarten as well as three sections each of Junior and Senior Kindergarten. Extended Day is available five days a week; parents have the choice of one to five days. In addition to new buildings, playgrounds, and multi-programs, many changes have occurred in the curriculum, but, as Kay states it, the curriculum "always maintains phonics, reading readiness, and math and science/social studies as the basis of the programs."

The knowledge that Kay was a successful Kindergarten teacher for many years enhances the respect teachers have for her. She works very closely with the Director of Admissions and meets many applicants with their parents before the girl is accepted at St. Mary's. Kay has a calm and quiet manner that attracts children to her and immediately makes them feel comfortable. She is especially

As Kay Humphreys talks about the Kindergarten program, one can feel her joy in the way the girls respond excitedly about learning. While she was visiting one class, she remembers hearing the students say, "Look, Mrs. Humphreys, we are doing our math and it's fun." She also enjoys reading their journals "where they had written in 'inventive spelling' using all consonants during their first semester," which demonstrates a progression in the language arts. The use of technology, and all its many resources, has greatly enhanced the program, but Kay emphasizes, "these are only tools of learning and do not replace the basics."

St. Mary's Express, Moss Hall.

Kay is impressed with her faculty and their dedication to teaching. She likes the way parents describe St. Mary's as "a home away from home, where the girls are given loving care." This, she stresses, "isn't a requirement of teachers; it is a 'given.'" Kay spends many hours talking with her faculty and is always ready to listen and counsel with them. After one of their many field trips, one of the cars filled with students didn't return for a considerable time after all the other girls had been deposited at the school. This worried everyone, of course, but as one teacher observed, "No one was in the state that Mother K was in." She is a mother to every Kindergarten child, and they all know her and love her.

interested in the student's correct placement in the Kindergarten program, for she realizes it has a vital effect on the remainder of the student's school and personal life. Her knowledge of the developmental age along with the intellectual age is invaluable to a student's success in school.

One of her teachers emphasizes, "She always manages to use the right words when talking to parents" and added, "She also has all the different facets important to being a fine administrator; she is a parent, a mother, a grandmother, and for years a teacher of young children." Another faculty member mentioned that Kay "is not only sympathetic to young children, but also very understanding with the faculty and their individual problems."

As Kindergarten is the first step to many years of a student's attending school, it is important that their introduction to an administrator be someone as gentle and caring as Kay Humphreys. When I picture her, I see her as the quintessence of quiet and peacefulness. She may be perturbed and upset, but rarely is this obvious to students or parents. She knows how to calm fears and encourage those around her to perform at their best. All of us at St. Mary's, particularly those at Moss Hall, are grateful for her presence here with us.

9. Preparation For The Next Century

Tom Southard

As each new Head has undertaken the responsibility of leading St. Mary's School, each one has been aware that this position presents a tremendous challenge. Although I was Acting Head for only one and one-half years, I remember the awesome weight that hung over me. After several conversations with Tom Southard, I was confident he knew the significance of the strength of this school and the necessity to guard it. This he has done with his eyes constantly open to improvements and changes necessary for St. Mary's growth and development. An outstanding faculty and staff, new buildings, a growing endowment fund, and an increasing number of students attest to his success.

Thomas Southard came to St. Mary's from Queen School in Upper Marlboro, Maryland, in July, 1987. Previously, he had been a Headmaster in the well-known Cathedral School of St. John the Divine, a K-8 school in New York City, and served as Headmaster of St. Michael's School and Assistant Head of St. Paul's School, both in Florida. A graduate of the University of South Carolina, he received an M.A. from the University of South Florida and worked on his doctorate in administration, planning, and supervision at the University of Alabama. In an interview shortly after he moved to Memphis, he remarked:

> I find the appointment an exciting opportunity. It is a challenge because St. Mary's already is a tremendously

Thomas N. Southard,
Headmaster since 1987.

successful school. My objective is to maintain and enhance that. Being the Headmaster of a Pre K-12 school had been my career ambition for a number of years … [It] was a professional dream come true.

In his *Recollections*, he remembers:

It was a 'snow day' in January of 1987, that I received a call from Bob Solmson, a member of the St. Mary's Episcopal School Search Committee. Perhaps no conversation in my life has been more life changing, challenging and fulfilling. After interviews with Walker Uhlhorn, Chairman of the

Among Tom's vivid memories is his first chapel at St. Mary's: Here I am, the man from the Episcopal school back east; I sat there weeping. Within me, before, during, and since that experience is the truth that my heart had a need for an outlet which before had been closed to the opportunity for genuine expression; I had to be all man at all times. The feminine within me now at this new moment had an outlet; it was immensely liberating. Since that day, I have been an evangelist for the benefits of an all girls' educational environment.

Search Committee, students, faculty, division heads, Dean Emerita, Mary Davis, Director of Development Madge Clark, and the Reverend Reynolds Cheney, Rector of the Church of the Holy Communion, I was offered the position. After discussions with my insightful wife, Edie, I enthusiastically accepted.

Having worked in Episcopal Schools since 1969, Tom realized the importance of his relationship with the Reverend Reynolds Cheney. Reynolds made it clear that his job was "to run the church" and my job was "to run the school." Tom also emphasized:

I felt Reynolds' support from the moment we talked and never has that relationship or sense of oneness been abridged. Geoff Butler was very helpful. His development of a strong and influential Board of Trustees, an outstanding faculty, an emphasis on endowment, a pre-campaign strategy to expand facilities at Moss Hall, and a commitment to diversity successfully positioned me for my first year at St. Mary's.

[This is an age] when parents are frequently consumed by the theory that happiness is a daily event and, in fact, not a natural outcome or consequence of a process called 'work,' I have found it increasingly more difficult to convince parents that the rigor underscoring a St. Mary's curriculum is the reason they should be investing in their daughter's education. Yet, in this world of creeping mediocrity, the enrollment at St. Mary's is at an all-time high. Come labor on! God does look over this place; His children need this place.

An early charge from the Board of Trustees was "to refine the campaign plan and raise significant amounts of money before going public." Tom's first year was helped immensely by John McQuiston, who continued as Board Chairman. Other leaders were Walker Uhlhorn, Chairman of the Construction Committee, and Chip and Tricia Dudley, Co-chairs of the Building Campaign, which raised $2.2 million dollars to provide additional classrooms, a new gymnasium, cafeteria, and ballet room housed in The Margaret R. Hyde Activity Center. The gymnasium became the Willmott Gymnasium as the result of a family gift from Peter Willmott, and the cafeteria and the ballet room was named the Starnes Common in honor of Mike Starnes, a major supporter of the campaign.

Margaret R. Hyde, Trustee and benefactor.

Madge Clark, Director of Development, knew the people to ask for monetary support; one was Margaret Hyde, Trustee Emerita, who was "a driving force on the Board of Trustees." In the midst of an intense Board meeting before going public, the Board was "reluctant to bite the bullet" about the amount of money needed. Silence fell in the room. It was at that moment that Miss Hyde said, "What are we waiting for? Let's do it." The Board immediately reacted by increasing their pledges. Thus began a period of tremendous growth at St. Mary's.

After improvement of buildings, Tom shifted his attention to the growth of the endowment fund. At the time of his arrival at St. Mary's, the endowment was slightly over one million dollars, a surprisingly low amount considering the many years of the school's existence. In the past 12-13 years, the endowment has increased tremendously, due to a challenge from Clarence Day. St. Mary's was challenged to raise $1,500,000 to be matched by $500,000 from the Day Foundation. Credit for emphasizing and increasing the endowment fund must be given to Mike McDonnell, a past trustee, and his leadership at the Board level, along with the energy of Geoff Butler. Gratitude needs to be expressed to Madge Clark, Director of Development, a supportive Board of Trustees led by Bob Solmson and later Tricia Dudley, for making it possible to meet this challenge. The current Worlds of Opportunity Campaign, a strong market, and the extraordinary management of the fund by Mason Hawkins, former trustee, CEO and Chairman of Southeastern Asset Management, has increased the endowment to $7,000,000. Since Madge Clark's resignation, a great deal of credit for this success goes to the creative ideas and hard work of Angie Gardner, Director of Development, and the other members of her department.

This fund has enlarged the average salary of the faculty, enhanced benefits, quadrupled money for need-based scholarships, and provided income that would otherwise have to come from tuition. The endowment fund has grown from $ 1.1 million in 1987 to approximately $7.0 million as of December 1997; the Annual Fund has increased 72% since 1991-92. Without this increase, we would not have been able to keep or recruit a faculty such as we continue to have. Nine years ago, a faculty member remarked, "We have been a cheap date too long!"

Mertie Buckman, who had been a contributor to the Margaret R. Hyde Chair of Excellence in the 1988 campaign, had remained in

Mertie Buckman, benefactor for whom Buckman Performing Arts Center was named, with granddaughter, Kathy Buckman Davis '80, and Mr. Southard.

close touch with the school. Mrs. Buckman is the grandmother of two St. Mary's alumnae—Kathy Buckman Davis '80 and Margaret Buckman '81. Her generosity made it possible to renovate and upgrade the Middle and Upper School science laboratory equipment with the thought that they could be moved to a new location when the school was able to build a science center.

It was during this period that Bob Solmson and Tom talked with Gayle and Mike Rose regarding their interest in building a theater at St. Mary's. As their talks continued, the needs of the school surpassed the original concept for a theater because of the growth of the student body and the tremendous success of the instrumental and choral music, art, and drama programs. The $700,000 project turned into a $5,000,000 major expansion.

The 1993-94 Chairman of the Board, Jim Warner, followed by Mike Farrow, provided strong leadership. The Worlds of Opportunity Campaign was launched in 1994 with Jim Taylor and Robin Formanek as Co-Chairs. The goal is $15,000,000; the initial stage raised nearly $7,000,000; $5,000,000 for the Buckman Center/Rose Theater and nearly $2,000,000 for endowment. This campaign is ongoing, and the hope is to raise the rest of the money for the endowment within the next three to five years.

Tremendous skepticism existed within the immediate school community about a girls' school in Memphis raising that amount of money. "No way," it was said, "could St. Mary's come close to raising

> *A school can only be as good as its faculty. From my first day on campus to the present, I have been moved by the fact that this faculty is the hardest working and most committed I have ever known. Working at St. Mary's is not a job, per se, for this faculty; it is instead a ministry dedicated to the education of girls and young women.*
>
> *—Tom Southard*

what a boys' school had raised, let alone exceed it." Fortunately for the school, the campaign was launched with an anonymous $1,000,000 gift; the largest single gift ever made to St. Mary's. The school began the public portion of the campaign with a gala under an enormous tent on the Lower School soccer field. In spite of everyone's efforts, it was slow going, with discouraging moments at first, but because of the immense generosity of Mrs. Mertie Buckman, the skeptics were silenced. Now, Tom's dream of having a building on the Middle and Upper School campus named for a woman and facing a building on the Lower School campus named for another exceptional woman, Margaret R. Hyde, became a reality.

He emphasizes one of his greatest concerns as Headmaster is to retain and to find the right teacher and person needed on this unique and sophisticated staff. The retirement of such teaching legends as Peggy O'Sullivan, Lee McMahon, Florence Curry, Jane Bradley, Anne Reiners, Lois Strock, and the resignations of Carmine Vaughan and Anne Fisher, along with the losses of Betty Lou Stidham and Faith Leonard, have presented the school some major challenges over the past ten years. The St. Mary's mark of excellence continues to perpetuate itself because of the tradition of excellence of each of these role models, and those who came before them.

Ever since his arrival in 1987, Tom has realized the strength of his administrative team. His association with Virginia Pretti is filled with vivid memories and great admiration. He states emphatically: "Without Virginia Pretti and her vast amount of knowledge, experience, wisdom and compassion, neither this school nor its Headmaster would be in the enviable positions they are today." On the lighter side, he remembers, "It was she who gave me my first lesson on the Macintosh computer which was on my desk when I arrived." He praises Anne Fisher, former Upper School Dean, "who was extraordinary in her ability to manage multiple priorities and was always a champion of academic excellence and the rigor which accompanies it. One of my worst moments as Headmaster at St. Mary's was receiving her letter of resignation."

He emphasizes that Kay Humphreys, Director of the Kindergarten:

> has been a tremendous catalyst in the growth, refinement, and sophistication of our Early Childhood Program ... Kay's softness combined with her strength and vast knowledge of child growth and development ... and ability to work with

Preparation for a concert: (standing) Barbara Carolino; (seated, left to right) Ann Wood, Emily Farrow, and Elizabeth Schatz. The Buckman Center and Rose Theater have become a major focal point for the arts to both the school and the community. Many people attend activities in the Center who otherwise would not become acquainted with St. Mary's. The Rose Theater has provided the space to house the wonderful programs created over the years by such outstanding fine arts and performing arts faculty as Anne Reiners, Rhendle Millen, Anne Anthony, Anne Fisher, Kate Davis, Julie Millen, Kay Betts, Louise Rooke, Joyce Gingold, and numerous others.

faculty, children, and parents ... is a major reason the Kindergarten has prospered.

Our Middle School Principal from 1984-1990, Emily Matheny, "demonstrated time and time again her ability to work with faculty, parents, and students with either academic, social, or emotional problems. Emily's decision to enter the priesthood was a loss to all of us."

Peggy Williamson, following Emily Matheny as Principal of the Middle School, "developed a deeply felt sense of purpose, esprit, and overall morale within her faculty. She is a highly organized, immensely thorough, and hands-on administrator." Following Anne Fisher's resignation, Gloria Weir was appointed Principal of the Upper School. Tom compliments her "on her hard work and commitment to St. Mary's at a transition time." She began a new position as

Director of Studies in 1996 and enjoys thoroughly her close association with the students on a daily basis.

Beginning in the fall of 1996, Dr. Gail Lewis became Principal of the Upper School, bringing a strong background in gifted education to our Upper School faculty, students, and families. Previously, she was the Middle School Principal of the Episcopal School Academy in Lafayette, Louisiana. "She has developed a meaningful and extremely important working relationship with large numbers of parents in the Upper School through monthly 'brown bag' lunches and other frequent times for interaction."

Because of the additional fundraising requirements placed upon Tom Southard, the nearly 25% increase in the student body since

Mr. Southard with Cheryl Sherrod, eighth grade graduation.

1987, and the sizable increase of demands on the time of the Assistant Head/Principal of the Lower School, the Board of Trustees approved the addition of another administrator beginning in the 1994-95 school year.

Virginia Pretti was promoted to Associate Head in addition to her position as Principal of the Lower School, and Keith Evans, previously Academic Dean at Webb School in Knoxville, accepted the position of Assistant Headmaster.

Keith Evans was introduced and recommended to Tom Southard by a former Headmaster of St. Mary's, the Reverend David Leech. Since his arrival, he has been given and has taken on many responsibilities. Tom believes

> [Keith's] exceptional intelligence and experience combined with an uncanny ability to handle multiple priorities with such calm and assuredness has enabled the School to explore and develop concepts and opportunities otherwise considered impossible.

Probably the biggest and most exciting change in 1997-98 has been the installation of a high speed Ethernet network with fiber optics, linking buildings, classrooms, and offices. This network provides access to the internet via a T-1 line. The school has four computer labs on campus, 250 computers, and employs six full-time technology specialists.

Linda Goodwin, Chair of Computer Science, with student.

Another new addition has been the installation of a SIRS (software) automated library system. What does all this technology mean to our students? It keeps students in touch with a wealth of information they would not have access to otherwise. They can press a key to visit a museum in England, observe students in a classroom in Russia, learn about animals by watching them perform in the San Diego Zoo, see historic events as they occur, and publish their own newspapers and magazines. As one sees the students glued to their computers, one can feel their excitement. It gives an added sparkle to their classroom work. The teachers, as well as the students, are thrilled with this new world, which continues to open around us.

Under Tom Southard's leadership, the school continues to thrive and to grow. The enrollment has increased 24% to 807 students, 15% of whom are of different cultures. An average of 40% of each year's graduating class are recognized by the National Merit Scholarship Program. Our students continue to be sought by the finest colleges because of their fine academic preparation. Tom has envisioned the school of tomorrow and made it possible for St. Mary's to adjust to the next century. When he first came to St. Mary's in 1987, he was interviewed by the *Memphis Business Journal*, in which he mentioned some of his dreams for the school; many have already been accomplished. The article also gives some personal information about him, which might not otherwise be known. It tells us how he listened to rock star, "The Boss," Bruce Springsteen, and watched the

Student Hala Khuri '97.

A member of his staff notes: Tom Southard somehow finds the time to do it all ... He is in touch with every aspect of school life, and that is what makes him such an effective Headmaster.

His success as a fund raiser has emerged naturally through the relationships he has developed and sustained with others who share his love for the school. A department head mentioned: Tom allows you to be creative in your department; he offers suggestions, encouragement and support on the road you decide to travel.

James B. Taylor, Jr., Chairman of the Board of Trustees, 1997-98.

music videos of "Ratt and Poison." Tom is quoted as saying, "One side of me wants to turn it off, and one side says, You better listen to it because it is what the generation in your school is listening to." The article continues: "[Southard] doesn't limit his pastimes to listening to rock music ... he also enjoys Beethoven, going to museums and the theater and watching football and basketball." In 1993, at the Upper School annual Christmas party, he dressed as Memphis' best known individual, Elvis Presley, and gave an outstanding performance to the delight of the faculty and the students.

On a more serious note, during the first fall Tom was here, one of the students recalls becoming acquainted with him on a rafting trip to the Ocoee River with the ninth grade and their dads. She remembers this time as "perhaps the most memorable and wonderful experience of my years at St. Mary's." Tom feels blessed to have the leadership and support of the Board of Trustees throughout his years here. They hold him in high esteem. One trustee touts:

> Tom sets a lofty standard for academic excellence, moral rectitude, compassionate discipline, and lively humor [and inspires] his faculty, the Board, and his students. He is the quintessential Headmaster to celebrate the Sesquicentennial of St. Mary's Episcopal School.

Board of Trustee Chairman, James B. Taylor, Jr., emphasizes:

> It is no small task to lead an institution with 150 years of tailwind behind it and yet know that the St. Mary's of 2020 will, and must, be different from the St. Mary's of 1970 ... Tom Southard possesses both a strong academic vision of how we must serve our students in the future and the substantial skills required to navigate the day to day course of educational life. With this exceptional combination of leadership qualities, he serves St. Mary's as both statistician and strategist, as both effective administrator and inspiring visionary.

Tom has worked hard to keep the standards high and to follow the traditions of St. Mary's. The added task of keeping the school abreast of all the developments in technology has required thought and persuasion. Tom listens to the opinions of his faculty and staff and considers them carefully, but inevitably, there comes that moment of decision to be faced alone. That time demands a courageous and caring individual. Tom has accepted the challenge of maintaining St. Mary's outstanding reputation.

Peggy Williamson

The journey that brought Peggy Williamson to St. Mary's Middle School in 1990 began at Southwestern in the 1960s. Her academic preparation as an English major influenced her to become a teacher and to study all the additional course work she needed to become one. She received an A.B. degree from Rhodes College in 1968 and her M.Ed. in Guidance and Personnel Services and Certification in Administration and Supervision from the University of Memphis in 1976. In 1981, Peggy received a Post- Master's Certificate from the University of Pennsylvania Graduate School. Her first teaching

Peggy Williamson, Middle School Principal, 1990 to present.

experience was in a junior high public school in Memphis. From there, she went to a large public high school in Norfolk, Virginia; then she taught at a suburban junior high school outside of Philadelphia, and from there to a center city Quaker school, Friends Select, in the same city. She moved back to Memphis and was offered a position in the CLUE program for the gifted child and held three different positions at the Memphis State University Campus School, first as counselor, second as curriculum director, and third as the Director of the School.

While she was Director of Campus School, her husband had an opportunity to return to Philadelphia, where Peggy pursued a program in family therapy at the University of Pennsylvania and the Philadelphia Child Guidance Center. When they returned to Memphis, she worked two years in the Children's Unit at Lakeside Hospital with children and their families. This background brought a wealth of experience and expertise to the position of Principal of the Middle School.

Except for one year in The Friend's Select School in Philadelphia, Peggy's teaching career had been entirely in public schools. Yet, according to her, "Immediately upon my arrival here, I realized I had truly found a very special place." Her husband often teases her about "why it took me so long to realize that St. Mary's was where I ought to work. Now, I recognize he was right!"

Several factors have led to her enthusiastic response, such as:

the numerous opportunities to work with students and families committed to excellence in education; the joy (of seeing) a fifth grader grow and mature over four years; the incredible warm and professional relationship with faculty.

Peggy adds, "These have been high points for me in my association with the school." She appreciates St. Mary's commitment to the individual potential of each student, for it

enhances this vital maturation process of young girls during the middle school years. During her years at St. Mary's, the school has held high the standards of excellence but has also encouraged the finding of new ways to unlock the talents of the students. The school now has a very valuable resource—a counseling coordinator for fifth through the twelfth grades and is looking for other resources in our hope to better serve the students.

Peggy, a native Memphian, says, "I had been aware of the fact that St. Mary's Episcopal School has always been synonymous with excellence." One of her aunts, Annah Lee Early, class of 1929, had talked about the superior education offered at St. Mary's. Her aunt emphasized two things that were very special to her about St. Mary's, which were "her excellent academic preparation and the friendships she made." Because of St. Mary's reputation and her aunt's high regard, Peggy was delighted to accept the offer to become Principal of the Middle School.

Peggy Williamson with students.

I was not surprised to discover that Peggy's faculty holds her in high esteem. Several mentioned her organizational ability and her knack of working with them as a team. One of the themes I heard frequently was her ability to build consensus and her talent for inspiring them to work cooperatively together. Another teacher remarked, "She is always professional in her dealings with the faculty, students, and parents. Although she has had a difficult day with many problems, she rarely loses her optimistic attitude." Her counseling training has proved helpful in dealing with the adolescents; she is well aware of the whole person.

One faculty member emphasized that Peggy takes "care of all the small details, so the teacher can concentrate on teaching." Although her goal for each student is learning, she realizes the need for students to be fed emotionally, spiritually, and physically.

Peggy has a surprising side to her that every once in a while appears. She has a dramatic flair that intrigues the students and faculty alike and adds fun and excitement to the life of the Middle School. Her password is "Cheers." We say "Cheers to her" for boosting her faculty with "Bravos" and for her understanding, wisdom, and diplomacy.

New Administrators in the '90s

Since the '90s began, St. Mary's has had three main developments that have brought about several noticeable changes in the school. One has been the enormous growth of technology, the second, the Worlds of Opportunity Campaign, which resulted in The Buckman Performing Arts Center and the Rose Theater, and the third, the changes in administration. The first two have already been mentioned, but I want to give special recognition to these administrators who came in the '90s and have added their expertise and dedication to the story of St. Mary's. By doing this, the story from 1847-1997 becomes complete.

The Reverend Mary Katherine Allman

In 1992, the Reverend Mary Katherine Allman was chosen to be our first Episcopal chaplain. Her B.A. and M.A. degrees were earned from Southwest State University and her Master of Divinity from The Episcopal Seminary of the Southwest. She was called in 1990 to be the Associate Rector of St. Mark's Episcopal Church in Corpus Christi, Texas, where she remained for two years before coming to St. Mary's. Her assignment was to plan and coordinate the chapel programs, to teach religion to the 7th, 9th, and 12th grades, and to serve as spiritual advisor to students and faculty.

This, Mary Katherine has accomplished, but she has also become involved with the students in their outreach programs including SMART, Tutoring for Excellence, and the Committee for Emphasis on Diversity. As a result of her association with them, the students affectionately call her "Rev." Her dedication to the acceptance of everyone as worthy of love and respect has influenced the entire school. Mary Katherine's homilies at chapel and special services are brief, meaningful, and always moving. Her voice rings out with conviction and leaves one feeling she lives close to God.

Mary Katherine has a fun-loving side which is delightful and makes us glad just to be alive. Her sense of humor and her wit accompany her constantly. She responded to my question about her years at St. Mary's by replying:

> St. Mary's is that rare kind of place that has the capacity to inspire and encourage everyone who has a connection to it,

The Reverend Mary Katherine Allman, Chaplain 1992-98.

to become a little better, try a little harder, and offer the best of herself to others. I will always consider the time I have been here to be above my life's most valued and cherished memories. I know that I am a better person for having had the chance to be a part of this school community.

The Reverend Allman left this past June to accept a two-year grant from the Pluralism Project at Harvard University. After completing this work, she will receive a Doctorate of Ministry from the Episcopal Divinity School in Cambridge, Massachusetts. St. Mary's is grateful for the years she has spent here. Daily, the students and faculty will miss her, but in their imaginations, she will be moving merrily over the countryside in her little blue Volkswagen or holding up traffic in Boston. Wherever she is, I am confident, in her unique and unexpected way, she will be spreading love and laughter wherever God leads her.

Keith Evans

Keith Evans came to St. Mary's in the fall of 1994 as Assistant Headmaster. He has an M.A. from Harvard University in administration and completed another master's degree in educational psychology at the University of Tennessee. Upon his arrival at St. Mary's, Keith remarked that he "was impressed with the students' positive attitude and focus." The other thing that attracted his attention was the quality of this faculty.

As Assistant Headmaster, his particular emphasis has been on working with the faculty through a variety of committees. His attitude is always positive and he has worked creatively with them, bringing to the school many new and creative ideas. In the past year, he has been teaching an elective course in psychology to the seniors. In a recent remark about the school, he emphasized:

> St. Mary's is a place that has set out to do more than the typical school. There is a real sense here that the business of the school is to provide a life changing experience for these students whether that is through the challenge of the curriculum, the athletic program or the emphasis on spiritual growth. That purpose inspires people to attempt what they might not otherwise do and to pull together to make the school really work for the good of the students.

The connection with the Episcopal Church was one of the most attractive aspects of this position. I particularly liked the fact that the school makes no apologies for being an Episcopal School, yet recognizes the importance of diversity. My sense is that the connection to the Church is of great value even to our students who come from different traditions.

—Keith Evans

Keith Evans, Assistant Headmaster, 1994 to present.

One of his special interests is his golf game. At the end of the year, he promoted a golf tournament among the teachers, which they thoroughly enjoyed—especially his final drive that veered off onto another hole which followed a succession of successful drives.

During these four years at St. Mary's, he has been diligent in all his endeavors. In talking about him, one of the Upper School teachers mentioned that Mr. Evans "is extremely intelligent and can converse on any subject. His soft spoken manner and graciousness make him very approachable."

As Assistant Headmaster, Keith has worked closely with Mr. Southard, assisting him in the many different facets of the school. His enthusiasm, dedication, and good humor are obvious assets to St. Mary's.

Gloria Weir

Gloria Weir has been associated with St. Mary's in many different ways since 1969, the year her daughter, Kendall '80, entered Kindergarten. Gloria earned her B.S. degree in Education and an M.A. in English from the University of Memphis. Often, as needs have arisen in the school, Gloria has responded graciously. I remember one of her first associations with students was teaching a "manners course." Since then, her list of responsibilities has been myriad: reading teacher, English teacher, Principal of the Upper School, and now, her present position as Director of Studies.

For a person who has been associated with St. Mary's as a parent, president of the Mother's Club, teacher and administrator, Gloria's comments are comforting:

> I have enjoyed every position I have had at St. Mary's. Whether in the role of parent, faculty member, or adminis-trator, I have experienced ... the dedication of all to create an atmosphere that supports a love of learning as well as excellence.

Her present position, as Director of Studies, gives her the "opportunity to work individually with the students in the Upper and Middle Schools." She has enjoyed this position, especially helping students make the transition from Lower to Middle, and then to Upper School.

Gloria's poise and good humor are evident in all her responsibil-ities. Her dedication to St. Mary's and her love of the school is visibly apparent. In her words, "St. Mary's is an exciting place to be every day." In our estimation, she has adapted to each of her positions with dedication and grace.

Gloria Weir, Director of Studies.

Gail Lewis

Gail Lewis, Principal of the Upper School, came to St. Mary's with impressive credentials. She received her B.A. degree from Carson-Newman College in Jefferson City, Tennessee, and her M.A. and Ed.D. from the University of Georgia. Her dissertation was *Hunger for Action: A Motivating Force in Creative Behavior and Juvenile Delinquency*. She has taught in several universities and high schools and came to St. Mary's from the Episcopal School of

Gail Lewis, Upper School Principal, 1996 to present.

Acadiana, where she was Head of the Middle School from 1992-1996.

Teachers and parents comment on her excellent ability as a public speaker. She speaks with both poise and clarity. Gail is a prolific writer and has been invited to present many papers at workshops and conferences, especially on the subject of the gifted child, which is her special interest. Her interesting and scholarly articles have been chosen for many educational journals. Gail's technical and natural talents in drama are appreciated by the faculty and students. Whenever Gail takes to the stage, the audience is in for a treat.

In response to my question about her feelings about St. Mary's, she responded:

> I have enjoyed the rich traditions surrounding the St. Mary's community like a comforting blanket. I especially love the ceremonies—like the crowning of the May Queen and graduation—that have been repeated by virtually every class since the school's founding. Those connections to the past provide us with grounding even as we leap headlong into the technological revolution and the 21st century.

Pursuits

Pursuits had its beginnings as a very small summer program in 1966, consisting of tennis and typing, along with courses offered in mathematics and English. Through a succession of creative and successful administrators, Anne Fisher, Camille Deaderick, Cherry Falls, Mary Pullen, Ph.D., Jan Davis, and Vicki Murrell, both the day camp and the offerings of academic courses increased yearly. The preparation for the SAT taught by Mary Hills Gill and Faith Leonard was always filled to capacity.

In 1988, Vicki Murrell became coordinator of auxiliary programs assisting the co-directors, Camille Deaderick and Cherry Falls in the financial and advertising facets of the summer program. During these years, the Drivers' Ed program was added. The program continued to grow rapidly and the name, Pursuits, was assigned to encompass all these activities. With the increasing importance of computer technology, there developed a need for a computer and publications director in the Upper and Middle schools. Vicki accepted this position in 1993.

*Sandra Pitts, Director of
Pursuits, 1993 to present.*

Fortunately at this time, Sandra Pitts applied for the position of Director of Pursuits. Her B.S degree was earned at Union University and her M.Ed. degree from the University of Memphis; she formerly taught at St. Agnes Academy. Sandra continued to introduce new and exciting opportunities for the students, such as overnight camps, trips to interesting sites in Memphis and other cities, multimedia shows, and many academic courses. Pursuits has become almost a school within a school. Everyone who works with her or near her recognizes her outstanding organizational and administrative ability.

The demand for these courses and events now requires a staff of twenty during the school year, and nearly fifty for the summer program. When school is in progress, the after school programs are limited to St Mary's students with an average attendance of 125. The summer activities are open to the public with an approximate enrollment of 500.

At St. Mary's, small beginnings have a way of growing into large and successful undertakings. Pursuits, with its excellent administrators, falls into this category. Each director has added her creative ideas making this program an outstanding one, giving a new dimension to the life of the school.

CONCLUSION

My task as a storyteller is completed. I have listened carefully to the reflections of St. Mary's leaders, teachers, alumnae, and students and no longer wonder why the school has lasted a century and a half despite its many difficulties. I believe it is because St. Mary's asks the best of us and challenges us to heights we did not know existed within us. This is the spirit of St. Mary's, and, as I hear the voices in this story speak, the sound of pride and joy in this place is clearly evident.

The journey I have traveled from 1847-1997 has been a long and heart-warming one. I have walked the muddy road to Hernando with Mary Pope; I have wept with Sister Constance and her companions; I have struggled through difficult times with Helen Loomis, Mary Paoli, and Katherine Neely; I have dreamed with Gilmore Lynn and Katharine Phillips; I have watched their dreams come true through the Headmasters and Principals who followed them, and I am grateful that I have been asked to travel with them. It is 1997 and my journey has come to an end. I leave the future with confidence in the hands of the many gifted leaders and teachers associated with the St. Mary's of today. May her story of love and faith survive another 150 years. Thanks be to God.

EPILOGUE

Many memorable events took place during our Sesquicentennial Year beginning with a birthday party, August 29, 1997, which included the entire school. This was followed October 16, 1997, by the dedication of two sculptures, the "Three Graces," honoring Mrs. Mertie Buckman, and "The Pillars of St. Mary's," honoring seven women: Mary Pope, the Sisters, Helen Loomis, Gilmore Lynn, Virginia Pretti, Mary Davis, Mertie Buckman, and Margaret Hyde. These women were the leaders and benefactors of the school. Maria Kirby-Smith '67 was the sculptor for both of these beautiful bronze art works. On that same day, the historical marker approved by the Tennessee Historical Commission on February 21, 1997, was unveiled by Paul Matthews and his daughter, Sarah, a member of the class of 2001.

Member of the Tennessee Historical Commission, Mr. Paul Matthews, and daughter, Sarah, class of 2001, in front of the marker approved by this commission on February 21, 1997.

Students in the play, Safely Home. *Standing (from left to right): Elizabeth James, Melissa Murray, Kim Fleishhauer, Allison Martin, Sister Lucy, Sister Margaret. Front: Ashley Bellet, Monica Wilson, Erin Wade, Mary Kathryn Millner.*

The moving performance of the play, *Safely Home*, written by the teachers, Sheila Patrick, Carol Lacy, Kate Davis, and several students, was produced in Rose Theater February 12-15. The play consisted of letters written by the Sisters to Mother Harriet in New York and captured the spirit of love and dedication demonstrated by the Sisters during the yellow fever epidemic. All who saw the play will forever be haunted by the beauty and commitment of the Sisters' lives even to the ultimate sacrifice of death of four of them by yellow fever.

On February 18, Dr. Joyce Brothers, psychologist and TV commentator, spoke to St. Mary's mothers and daughters about their special relationships. The final celebration, May 14, 1998, honored all the former living Headmasters of the school: Dr. Nathaniel C. Hughes, Mrs. Mary Davis, the Reverend David Leech, Mr. Geoffrey C. Butler, and the present Headmaster, Mr. Thomas N. Southard.

Although Mary Pope, the school's founder, was buried at Elmwood Cemetery with her family, her grave did not have a marker. The decision was made to rectify this. This headstone was made possible by the generous gifts of the class of 1997, the former Headmasters, and the current Headmaster. The Reverend Mary Katherine Allman conducted the ceremony. I believe it would have pleased Mary Pope, for it was in accord with her wishes as expressed in her poem, "Oh When This Fevered Life is O'er!" read by Dr. Hughes. The Blessing was given by The Right Reverend James M. Coleman, Bishop, Diocese of West Tennessee.

Mary Foote Pope's Tombstone with Headmaster's the Reverend David Leech, Thomas N. Southard, Mary M. Davis, Dr. Nathaniel C. Hughes, Jr., and Geoffrey C Butler.

The formal presentation of the tombstone by the class of 1997 was made by Autumn Witt. The observance concluded with the offering of roses by Piper Gray, class of 2004, and other descendants of the Pope family, Mrs. Mildred Highleyman, Mrs. Angeline Pittman, Ms. Kelly Micheel, and Mrs. Leesa Gilliard. The St. Mary's School Prayer, and the hymn, "Day by Day" brought to a close this significant and historic ceremony.

A dinner at Memphis Brooks Museum of Art presided over by James B. Taylor, Jr., Chairman of the Board of Trustees, climaxed the celebration. Each Headmaster was toasted by the Chairman of the Board during his/her tenure and responses were made by each one. The gifts of a St. Mary's chair and a framed picture including their pictures as well as that of former Principal, Mrs. Gilmore Lynn,

*The present and past
Headmasters of St. Mary's at the
Sesquicentennial Celebration.*

painted by Karen Adams Tosi '82, was given to each of them. A
highlight of the evening was the ovation and gift honoring Fannie
Warr, devoted employee, for her thirty years of outstanding service to
St. Mary's. Also honored with gifts were Bucky Hughes, Evie Butler,
and Edie Southard, wives of the Headmasters. As Mrs. Lynn could
not be present because of ill health, her daughter, Mary Catherine
Lynn Hitchings '47, received the gift in her place. We are indebted to
all who made it a never-to-be-forgotten evening recalling associations and events through the years and evoking many humorous and
cherished memories. One Headmaster remarked, "Ever since I left St.
Mary's, I have remembered this as a place where I felt surrounded
by love."

BIBLIOGRAPHY

—. *The Sisters of St. Mary at Memphis: With the Act and Sufferings of the Priests and Others Who Were There with Them during the Yellow Fever Season of 1878.* New York, 1879.

Capers, Jr., Gerald M. *The Biography of a River Town: Memphis: Its Heroic Age.* New Orleans: Tulane University, 1966.

Coppock, Paul R. *Paul R. Coppock's Mid-South.* Edited by Helen M. Coppock and Charles W. Crawford. Memphis: West Tennessee Historical Society, 1985.

Crawford, Charles W. *Yesterday's Memphis.* Miami: E.A. Seeman Publishing, 1976.

Davies-Rodgers, Ellen. *The Great Book: Calvary Protestant Episcopal Church: 1832-1972.* Memphis: The Plantation Press, 1973.

Davis, John H. *St. Mary's Cathedral: Centennial History, 1858-1958.* Memphis: Chapter of St. Mary's Cathedral, 1958.

Harkins, John E. *Metropolis of the American Nile: An Illustrated History of Memphis and Shelby County.* Edited by R. J. Bedwell and Trent Booker. Oxford, Mississippi: Guild Bindery Press, 1982.

Hilary, Sister Mary, CSM. *Ten Decades of Praise: The Story of the Community of Saint Mary during its first Century: 1865-1965.* Racine, Wisconsin: Dekoven Foundation, 1965.

Lynn, Gilmore Bicknell, ed. *History of St. Mary's Episcopal School: 1943-1975*. Memphis, 1996.

Meriwether, Elizabeth Avery. *Recollections of 92 Years: 1824-1916*. Nashville: Tennessee Historical Foundation, 1958.

Tardy, Mary T. *Southland Writers, Biographical and Critical Sketches of Living Female Writers of the South with Extracts from their Writings by Ida Raymond* (pseud). Philadelphia: Claxton, Remsen and Haffelfinger, 1870.

Sigafoos, Robert A. *Cotton Row to Beale Street: A Business History of Memphis*. Memphis: Mempis State University Press, 1979.

Wedell, Marsha. *Elite Women and the Reform Impulse in Memphis, 1875-1915*. Knoxville: University of Tennessee Press, 1991.

APPENDIX

Heads of the School

Mary Foote Pope	1847-1872
Sisters of the Order of St. Mary	1873-1910
Helen Loomis/Mary Paoli	1910-1922
Helen Loomis/Katherine Neely	1922-1949
Gilmore Lynn	1949-1958
Lawrence Lobaugh	1958-1962
Dr. N.C. Hughes, Jr.	1962-1973
Mary M. Davis (Acting Head)	1973-1974
The Reverend David Leech	1974-1980
Mary M. Davis (Acting Head)	Second Semester-1981
Geoffrey C. Butler	1981-1987
Thomas N. Southard	1987-present

Principals

Lower School:

Leonard Sewell	1872-1873
Gilmore Lynn	1958-1975
Katharine Phillips	1975-1980
Madelyn Brock (Acting)	1980-1982
Mary Williams	1982-1984
Virginia Pretti	1984-present

Middle School:

Camille Deaderick	1978-1984
Emily Matheny	1984-1990
Peggy Williamson	1990-present

Upper School:

Helen Allen	1962-December 1963
Katharine Phillips (Acting)	2nd Semester-1964
Mary M. Davis (Dean)	1964-December 1978
Virginia Pretti	1979-1984
Anne Fisher	1984-1994
Gloria Weir	1994-1996
Dr. Gail Lewis	1996-present

1997-1998 Board of Trustees

First Board of Trustees — 1958

Officers:

> George P. Phillips, Chairman
> Robert M. McRae, Vice Chairman
> Jean H. Cone, Secretary
> A.L. Whitman, Treasurer

Board Members:

> Lorin B. Allen
> Arthur C. Best
> Edmond B. Greenhaw
> Marvin W. Lathram, Jr.
> Joseph Orgill, Jr.
> Richard Overman
> Harry E. Schadt
> Walter P. Sprunt, Jr.
> Janet G. Tate
> Mercer E. West, III
> William N. Wilkerson

Chairmen — Board of Trustees 1958-1997

1958-62 — George P. Phillips
1962-64 — Harry Schadt
1964-66 — Al Whitman
1966-68 — Newton Allen
1968-70 — John T. Fisher
1970-72 — James L. Fri
1972-74 — Thomas F. Johnston
1974-76 — John Cawthon
1976-78 — Roy Bell, Jr.
1978-80 — Thomas M. Garrott, III
1980-82 — Robert Fogelman
1982-83 — James Barksdale
1983-85 — Ms. Barbara Keathley
1985-86 — Peter Willmott
1986-88 — John McQuiston
1988-91 — Robert Solmson
1991-93 — Mrs. Patricia N. Dudley
1993-94 — James Warner
1994-97 — J. Michael Farrow
1997-98 — James B. Taylor, Jr.

Mother's Club Presidents

1955-56 — Janet Pryor; Louise McRae (Temporary Chair)
1956-57 — Janet Tate
1957-58 — Jean Cone
1958-59 — Virginia von Lackum
1959-60 — Lucille Watkins
1960-61 — Brenda Heller
1961-62 — Betty Locke
1962-63 — Margaret Tenent
1963-65 — Martha York
1965-66 — Barbara Boehme
1966-67 — Betty Bledsoe
1967-68 — Norma Stroud
1968-69 — Ann Higginbotham
1969-70 — Ada Cockroft
1970-71 — Chris Garrett
1971-72 — Bobbie Goforth
1972-73 — Susan Burton
1973-74 — Kelsey Brooks
1974-75 — Nina Wilson
1975-76 — JoAnne Tilley
1976-77 — Gloria Weir
1977-78 — Tandy Gilliland
1978-79 — Sandy Sherman
1979-80 — Lynn Holloway
1980-81 — Ginia Vookles
1981-82 — Pat Crumrine
1982-83 — Judy Dixon
1983-84 — Carol Richardson

Parent's Association

1984-85 — Ann Stanley
1985-86 — Diane Mays
1986-87 — Diane Laster
1987-88 — Punk Davidson
1988-89 — Judy Nokes
1989-90 — Irwin Zanone
1990-91 — Libba Schatz
1991-92 — Gayle Bourland
1992-93 — Anita Burkett
1993-94 — Beverly Finnell
1994-95 — Rosanne Anderson
1995-96 — Susan Liddon
1996-97 — Diane Williams
1997-98 — Carla Carter

Faculty and Staff 1949-1998
(Either present faculty or at St. Mary's five years or more)

Sylvia Adams, Helen Allen, the Reverend Mary Katherine Allman, Mrs. Oscar Ammer, Alberta Anderson, Dr. Emmett Anderson, Anne Anthony, Marcelle Askew, Lorraine Ausprich, Lee Avant

Andy Banks, Doris Bard, Lola Barkow, Kueilan Barnes, Peggy Barrett, Betty Jane Barringer, Sydney Bates, Ann Bendall, Cathy Bennett, Marilyn Benny, Nancy Bethell, Kay Betts, Rita Bielskis, Susan Bingham, Nancy Blair, Elizabeth Boggs, Penny Bower, Jane Bradley, Trula Branon, Laura Brewer, James Brinson, Madelyn Brock, Rick Broer, Judy Brundige, Joan Burr, Bede Burr, Geoffrey C. Butler

Linda Cannon, Jennifer Cantrell, Tania Castroverde, Patricia Chambliss, Madge Clark, Allison Brown Coates, Betty Coleman, Deborah Condry, Ann Humphreys Copp, Mrs. C.L. Cox, Elaine Cox, Jean Croye, Florence Curry, Charles Curtiss

Ann Dailey, Joan Daniel, Jan Cone Davis, Kate Davis, Mary Davis, Camille Patterson, Deaderick, Phoebe Dent, Gay Dickinson, Cynthia Dickson, Liz Ann Dinkelspiel, Cherie Dowd, Patricia Dudley

Lynn Edwards, Mary Lou Entzminger, Laurel Eskridge, Emilie Evans, Cathy Evans, Keith Evans

Cherry Falls, Margaret Fayssoux, Helen Fentress, Anne Fisher, Josephine Flexner, Sarah Loaring-Clark Flowers, Alice Franceschetti, Shelley Fraser, Jeffrey Fry, Zoe Futris

Wendy Gallik, Elizabeth Garat, Angie Gardner, David Gardner, Carolyn George, Mary Hills (Presh) Gill, Joyce Gingold, Bobbie Goforth, Jean Anne Goodson, Linda Goodwin, Marilyn Gordon, Virginia Gordon, Suzanne Goza, Dianne Gregory, Mimi Grossman

Marion West Hammer, Betty Jane Harris, Sallie Harris, Betty Harrison, Rebecca Haskell, Paige Henson, Carolyn Heppel, Shelley Herzke, Suzanne Hillis, Mary Catherine Lynn Hitchings, Chrystal Hogan, Katherine House, Gaye Lynn Huddleston, Julia Hughes, Bucky Hughes, Jeanne Hughes, Dr. Nathaniel Cheairs Hughes, Jr., Kay Humphreys

Carol Irwin

Becky Jacks, Shannon Jarchow, Kempie Craddock Jenkins, Susan Jones

Rodney Keith, Patty Kelly, Harold Ketchersid, Janice Kilpatrick, Janet Kimmy, Martha Kittrell, Kelly Klinke, Pat Knight, Deborah Kuykendall

Carol Lacy, Holly Land, Elizabeth Lansing, Faith Leonard, the Reverend David Leech, Dr. Gail Lewis, Lester Liebengood, Lawrence C. Lobaugh, Melissa Lofton, Gilmore Lynn, Betty Lyon, Lynda Lyttle

Kathleen Mainardi, Nancy Whitman Manire, Barbara Mansberg, Leigh Mansberg, Rachel Martin, Emily Matheny, Martha May, Mimi McCracken, Billy McDaniel, Steve McDaniel, Kathleen McElroy, Pat McKibben, Gwenice McLaughlin, Karen McLaughlin, Lee McMahon, Mike McWilliams, Shirley Metcalfe, Linda Middlecoff, Julia Millen, Dr. Rhendle Millen, Jeanne Stevenson-Moessner, Suzanne Montgomery, Stella Moody, Mary Frances Moore, Mrs. Paul W. Moore, Marilou Mulrooney, Grace Murdoch, Kathryn Murphy, Vicky Murrell

Sally Navarra, Mavis Negroni, Judy Nokes

Elizabeth Oehmler, Peggy O'Sullivan

Allison Wellford Parker, Mrs. A.D. Parker, Carolyn Parrish, Sheila Patrick, Kathy Daniel Patterson, Mignon Payne, Peggy Perkins, Evelyn Perry, Ann Petersen, Beverly Peterson, Jill Peterson, Katharine Phillips, Cynthia Pitcock, Michael Pitts, Sandra Pitts, Anita Pohlman, Kira Pollack, Birdie Pope, Virginia Pretti, Nancy Prillaman, Ann Driscoll Prince, Dr. Mary Pullen

Nanette Quinn

David Ramsey, Allyson Raymer, Julene Reed, Julie Reeves, Anne Reiners, Mrs. A.W. Rogers, Tricia Rohr, Louise Rooke, Betty Ruleman, Sharon Rutledge

Libba Schatz, Steve Shahan, Jane Shelton, Traci Sherman, Betsy Siler, Betty Lou Stidham, Dr. Mark Slovak, Marisa Smalley, Barbara Smith, Susan Whitten Snodgrass, Barbara Snyder, Thomas N. Southard, Jean Stanfield, Marsha Stemmler, Mrs. Horace Stepp, Maxine Stevens, Cindy Strock, Lois Strock

Richard Tanner, Susan Taylor, Lisa Team, Louise Terry, Francie Thurman, Emily Townes, Joan Traffas

Barbara Umfress

Carmine Vaughan, Barbara Viser

Josie Walker, Fannie Warr, Gloria Weir, Yolande Welch, Tony Whicker, Sharon Whitaker, Joanna Wilcox, Lindy Williams, Sue Williams, Peggy Williamson, Ann Wiseman, Jeanne Wilson, Ann Wright

Mandy Yandell

Morgan Zanone, Charlotte Zehring

Council of Advisors 1996-1997

Chairman: Dr. Cynthia Pitcock
Mrs. William J. Adams
Mr. A.D. Alissandratos
Mr. Newton P. Allen
Ms. Jekka Ashman '78
Mrs. Gwen Awsumb '32
Mr. Fred K. Beeson
Mrs. Harriette Beeson '53
Mrs. Arthur C. Best
Mrs. James A. Breazeale
Mr. L. Palmer Brown, III
Mrs. Mertie W. Buckman
Mr. John R. Cawthon
Mrs. H. Douglas Chism '36
Mrs. Ross B. Clark, II
Mr. Sam Cooper
Mr. Jack J. Craddock
Mrs. Charles M. Crump
Mr. Barney L. DuBois
Mr. John T. Fisher
Mrs. Jill Flournoy '70
Mrs. Sarah Flowers '47
Mr. Robert Fogelman
Mr. James H. Frazier
Mr. James L. Fri, Jr.
Dr. Christine Garrett
Mr. Thomas M. Garrott, III
Mrs. Tandy Jones Gilliland
Mr. Lester Gingold
Mr. Louis H. Haglund
Mr. O. Mason Hawkins
Mr. Henry R. Heller
Mrs. Sarah Hodges '73
Mr. Lewis E. Holland
Mr. Joseph R. Hyde, III
Mrs. Carroll Johnson
Mr. Thomas F. Johnston
Mr. Frank A. Jones, Jr.
Dr. Andrew H. Kang
Ms. Carol Sue Keathley '64
Mrs. Barbara P. Keathley
Mrs. William F. Kirsch, Jr.
Mrs. John R. Lynn
Mr. B. Lee Mallory, III

Mrs. Barbara W. Mansberg
Mr. Michael McDonnell
Mr. John W. McQuiston, II
Dr. Musette Morgan '72
Ms. Brooke A. Morrow '74
Mrs. E. Eric Muirhead
Mrs. Carol Murff Oates
Mr. Joseph Orgill, III
Mrs. William F. Outlan
Ms. Hallie L. Peyton '82
Mr. John B. Peyton
Mrs. George P. Phillips
Mr. Harry Phillips
Mrs. Weetie Phillips
Mr. Joseph H. Powell
Mrs. Janet Pryor '34
Dr. Patti Person Ray '65
Mr. S. Herbert Rhea
Ms. Lila Saunders
Mr. Arthur N. Seessel, III
Mr. William King Self, Jr.
Mr. Robert M. Solmson
Mr. John W. Stokes, Jr.
Mr. Dan B. Turley, Jr.
Mr. Walker Uhlhorn
Mrs. Chalmers Valentine '80
Mr. James C. Warner
Mr. Ben F. Whitten, Jr.
Mr. and Mrs. Harry J. Phillips

Outstanding Teachers

1964 — Julia Hughes
1965 — Peggy O' Sullivan
1966 — Shelley Fraser
1967 — Mary Hills Baker Gill
1968 — Maxine Stevens
1969 — Carolyn Parrish
1970 — Anne Reiners
1971 — Betty Lou Stidham
1972 — Lee McMahon
1973 — Helen Fentress
1974 — Florence Curry
1975 — Sydney Bates
1976 — Barbara Mansberg
1977 — Betsy Siler
1978 — Mary Davis
1979 — Sylvia Adams
1980 — Louise Rooke
1981 — Anne Fisher
1982 — Madelyn Brock
1983 — Judy Morgan
1984 — Faith Leonard
1985 — Cherry Falls
1986 — Carmine Vaughan
1987 — Joan Burr
1988 — Lois Strock
1989 — Judy Brundige
1990 — Camille Deaderick
1991 — Carol Lacy
1992 — Ann Bendall
1993 — Mary Pullen
1994 — Betty Jane Barringer
1995 — Sue Williams
1996 — Mary Lou Mulrooney
1997 — Debbie Kuykendall
1998 — Mary Davis

Outstanding Alumnae

1992 — Lee McGeorge Durrell '67
1993 — Jeanne Stevenson-Moessner '66
1994 — Cristina Brescia Michta '70
1995 — Jan Muirhead '71
1996 — Gwen Robinson Awsumb '32
1997 — Brooke Morrow '74
1998 — Nora Wingfield Tyson '75

Student Council Presidents

1960-61 — Beverly Burkett
1961-62 — Penny Lougheed
1962-63 — Evelyn Perry
1963-64 — Ann Humphreys
1964-65 — Julia Malone
1965-66 — Jeanne Stevenson
1966-67 — Lee McGeorge
1967-68 — Libby Wetter
1968-69 — Marta Richards
1969-70 — Lynn Schadt
1970-71 — Julia Sprunt
1971-72 — Ashley Moore
1972-73 — Ellen Clark
1973-74 — Kristi Hoffman
1974-75 — Margaret Flowers
1975-76 — Crissy Garrett
1976-77 — Molly Townes
1977-78 — Carol Fri
1978-79 — Anne Beeson
1979-80 — Jamie Feild
1980-81 — Ellen Feild
1981-82 — Meg Beeson
1982-83 — Karen Griffith
1983-84 — Clare Halle
1984-85 — Margaret Frazier
1985-86 — Kay Seessel
1986-87 — Lauren Moran
1987-88 — Leigh Vaughan
1988-89 — Tiffany Perel
1989-90 — Miriam Kriegel
1990-91 — Margaret Craddock
1991-92 — Alexis West
1992-93 — Leigh Weinberg
1993-94 — Sophie Askew
1994-95 — Vanessa Buch
1995-96 — Mamie Tinkler
1996-97 — Abby Taylor
1997-98 — Amy Sellers

Honor Council Presidents

1970-71 — Marty Jones
1971-72 — Kathy Watson
1972-73 — Terry Maguire
1973-74 — Brooke Morrow
1974-75 — Watty Brooks
1975-76 — Lucy Loveless

1976-77 — Vicki Snyder
1977-78 — Christy Smith
1978-79 — Corinne Johnson
1979-80 — Nancy Carlson
1980-81 — Mollie McCarroll
1981-82 — Camille LeMaster, Elizabeth Simpson
1982-83 — Bonnie Bolton
1983-84 — Leslie Darling
1984-85 — Becky Stratton
1985-86 — Kim Malone
1986-87 — Anne McCarroll
1987-88 — Margaret Malone
1988-89 — Maysey Craddock
1989-90 — Paige Russell
1990-91 — Rachel Kiefer
1991-92 — Wendy Sacks
1992-93 — Veena Paidipalli
1993-94 — Carolyn Porter
1994-95 — Hallie Bourland
1995-96 — Bernice Chen
1996-97 — Hallye Ferguson
1997-98 — Katie Broer

Alumnae Presidents

1939-40 — Betty Thompson Russell, Acting Chairman
1964-65 — Betty Witsell
1967-68 — Mary Katherine Lynn Hitchings
1968-69 — Sarah Loaring-Clark Flowers
1969-70 — Marguerite Joyner
1970-71 — Margaret Loaring-Clark Jones
1971-72 — Iolis Robbins Carruthers
1972-73 — Kay Allenberg Cohen
1973-75 — Linda Avery Reaves
1975-76 — Nancy Whitman Manire
1976-77 — Ann Humphreys Copp
1977-78 — Harriette Mathewes Beeson
1978-79 — Bette West Bush
1979-80 — Jill Tanner Flournoy
1980-81 — Jean Phillips Lorton
1981-82 — Jill Schaeffer Broer
1982-84 — Ashley Moore Mayfield
1984-87 — Brooke Morrow
1987-90 — Ginny Waller Zanca
1990-92 — Sarah Peeples Hodges
1992-94 — Chalmers Peyton Valentine
1994-96 — Hallie Peyton
1996-98 — Mary Kavanagh Day

St. Mary's May Queens

1891 — Ann Blanche Steele
1907 — Elizabeth Brinkley
1910 — Lucia Burch
1917 — Annette Mason
1920 — Josephine Hyde
1921 — Grace Eleanor Griffith
1925 — Margaret Blackburn
1929 — Anne Galbreath
1930 — Margaret Newton
1931 — Alice McKee
1932 — Anne Brown Taylor
1933 — Frances Portlock
1934 — Doris Warr
1935 — Nancy Donelson
1937 — Marianne McKellar
1938 — May Louise Ingram
1940 — Cynthia Ann Hobbs
1941 — Helen Shawhan
1942 — Trudy Bruce
1945 — Jeannie Botto
1946 — Carolyn Cranford
1947 — Pauline Fisher
1948 — Iolis Robbins
1949 — Florence Batchelor
1961 — Linda Avery
1962 — Penny Lougheed
1963 — Patty Ozier
1964 — Phyllis Kohler
1965 — Cathryn Hoover
1966 — Charlotte Dabbs
1967 — Libba Mann
1968 — Libby Wetter
1969 — Nora Heflin
1970 — Ruthie Stratton
1971 — Happy Stratton
1972 — Meg Jemison
1973 — Elizabeth Hughes
1974 — Sharon Russell
1975 — Louisa Page
1976 — Cristen Garrett
1977 — Alicia Harwood
1978 — Margot Bell
1979 — Frances Crenshaw

1980 — Chalmers Peyton
1981 — Mollie McCarroll
1982 — Hallie Peyton
1983 — Brandon Garrott
1984 — Kelly O'Shields
1985 — Nicco Anderson
1986 — Carolyn Oates
1987 — Anne McCarroll
1988 — Beth Gowen
1989 — Tiffany Perel
1990 — Paige Russell
1991 — Tish Dudley
1992 — Alexis West
1993 — Bethany Mays
1994 — Mary Denton
1995 — Allison McConomy
1996 — Katie Kuykendall
1997 — Katie Broer
1998 — Annie McLaren

St. Mary's May Princesses

1956 — Anne Ellis
1957 — Adrienne Morgan
1958 — Katharine Phillips
1959 — Evelyn Perry
1960 — Susan McRae
1961 — Ann Marmon
1962 — Margaret Jeanne Whitman
1963 — Jeannette DuBignon Cone
1964 — Julie Bond
1965 — Ruthie Stratton
1966 — Nancy and Elizabeth Johnson
1967 — Mary Leatherman
1968 — Margaret Erb
1969 — Leigh Haizlip
1970 — Martha Flowers
1971 — Kathleen Person
1972 — Alicia Harwood
1973 — Margot Bell
1974 — Christy Britt
1975 — Jeanne Burrow
1976 — Sarah Burton
1977 — Laura Scholes
1978 — Suzanne McCloy
1979 — Clare Halle
1980 — Lisa Breazeale
1981 — Carol Mosely
1982 — Pattra Summers
1983 — Beth Gowen
1984 — Ashley Moore
1985 — Martha Roberson
1986 — Jennifer Breazeale
1987 — Mary McDonnell
1988 — Bethany Mays
1989 — Mary Denton
1990 — Gabrielle Rose
1991 — Betsy Robinson
1992 — Jami Richards
1993 — Erin Wade
1994 — Sidney Hawkins
1995 — Ragan Stout
1996 — Sarah Matthews
1997 — Christina Leatherman
1998 — Musette Morgan

INDEX

A moment of levity in a 1978 art class.